About the Author

Christine is a wife, and mother of three grown-up children and has five grandchildren. She has been married to Chris for 43 years.

The daughter of a minister she played a major part in her parents' ministry. She married Chris, a minister's son who also played a part in his parent's ministry.

In the 1960's Chris and Christine toured England as *'Kris & Kristine - The Sunshine Evangelists.'* Christine was a children's evangelist during this period.

In 1970 they received a unique call to take the gospel to cave-dwelling people in a remote part of Spain.

In 1990 they founded The Midlands Bible College, England. Their eldest son is now the Director.

In 1994 Christine established the first European branch of the Full Gospel Fellowship of Churches and Ministers International, building up a membership of over one hundred ordained ministers in a year.

In 1999 Christine had a burden to open an Evangelical English-speaking church service in a spiritually barren region of Southern Spain. It was the very first and her vision inspired a spin-off of several fellowships in surrounding areas meeting the needs of a large English speaking expatriate community.

Lost In Faith

By Christine Smith

It Could Take Faith... to

Devotional Publishing Ltd

Copyright © Christine Smith 2009

ISBN 978-0-9560078-0-3

A catalogue record for this book is available from the British
Library.

Printed in Great Britain by
York Publishing Services Ltd

Devotional Publishing Ltd
Kemp House
152-160 City Road
London
EC1V 2NX

Orders: www.lostinfaith.org

Contents

1

It Could Take Faith…

to walk all alone

I am crushed with despair and emptiness on the realization of what we have done. How could we have brought our two little English boys to live in such a snake-ridden, fly-infested, barren, and scorched filthy wilderness? I go weak at the knees and slump down to sit on a rock unable to hold back sobs, staring at nothing less than a time warp. "Christine, I'm so sorry I brought you here," Chris, my husband is saying, taking my hand and holding it gently in his. "Listen, I'll take you home tomorrow sweetheart, and we'll forget all about gypsies, caves, a life of faith, and being missionaries, and I really mean it."

I am too English. England is a life of comfort on a well populated clean, neat, and green island. Yet all the normal things about my country have hit me for the first time ever, as having been heaven, yet were simply asphalted roads, neatly formed houses, and street lamps. I'd never realized until this moment, that even the basic of gadgets in my house had been domestic bliss.

I was the youngest of four daughters. How my Dad longed for the fourth to be a boy, really craving a son. But on August 31st 1944 in Mom and Dad's house at Dixons Green, Dudley, I arrived. The midwife had kept going downstairs to keep my Dad informed of Mom's progress. Dad paced the hallway waiting anxiously for the announcement that his son had arrived. But then the dreaded words of the midwife were heard… "It's another girl!"

My Dad exclaimed… "No, not *another* girl!"

The midwife piped up, "You naughty man Mr Middleton."

I was named Christine and Dad adored and spoiled me. My life was a life of plenty; the only daughter to benefit from the success of a business Dad had worked years to build up.

It seemed that I could have almost anything I wanted, yet not without a comment from my three older sisters how things hadn't been like that for them. I could sense how it comforted Mom and Dad to see the desire I had for spiritual things, as they painfully watched my three sisters' decline from it.

We all lived in a spacious detached house. Then Dad even bought another house; a bungalow by the beach in Prestatyn, North Wales. Having two houses in 1960, meant we were viewed as a wealthy family.

My life was made leisurely and undemanding by my sweet, devoted, Christian-living Mom who took me on regular shopping sprees. The bags I carried home every Saturday, spilling over with fancy new outfits, weren't treats to me, but a normal weekend. Every day Mom made it her business to ask what I fancied to eat. I was a fussy eater and especially loathed vegetables, so there were never any on my plate. It was mostly the best cuts of meat, and Mom's perfectly roasted potatoes and delicious gravy. Nothing was too much trouble for Mom regarding her children. No household duty had any part in my life whatsoever. Mom believed it was her job as a Mom to wait on us all hand and foot. Sometimes my Auntie Mary came around to help in the home, but it was only because she was a needy sister of Mom's, so it was Mom's way of giving her a little job.

My Dad often joked about how married life could be tough for me, because of my easy life, and laughed that my husband would end up starving because I wouldn't even know how to boil him an egg. But nothing changed. Mom and Dad never required much from any of us. They only wanted to make life good for their offspring.

On one particular shopping spree alone I arrived home with a solid gold watch, a wide engraved silver bangle, and a pearl ring. The pearl ring was special. It was due to a famous American evangelist called Clifton Erickson who was scheduled to preach at the Birmingham Town Hall. An American coming to speak in Birmingham in the 1960s was a huge and exciting event and everyone talked of nothing else for months. There was even more excitement once we knew that the evangelist's womenfolk were to accompany him. So we had extra special new outfits for the occasion. Everyone in the Town Hall had their eyes fixed in delight on the ladies' extraordinary fancy clothes, shoes, jewellery, and especially their massive lacquered bouffant hairstyles, bright make-up… and even earrings! We had never seen the likes of it, and although we were delighted, we were also confused about the make-up and earrings, having had it drummed into us how it was a worldly practice. Nevertheless, it seemed to be forgiven as 'Americanism.' We couldn't wait for the congregational singing to be over

– which was normally the most enjoyable part of a service for us – so that we could hear the evangelist speak. His big confident accent would make us feel as if we were in the presence of John Wayne or some other film star. I was sitting near to the evangelist's daughter at the front, having been at the Town Hall early, queuing on the street to get the best seats. I could spot the gorgeous pearl ring she was wearing. The very next week Mom took me shopping until we found a pearl ring as similar as we could find to the one the evangelist's daughter had. Although Mom had taken me to Dudley, Wolverhampton, and Birmingham to find the biggest pearl available, we were unable to find one as big as the evangelist's daughter's. But my pearl ring gave me a taste of American glamour whenever I wore it on a special occasion.

One day, in one of Dad's shops in Castle Street, Roseville, Coseley, which was a mix of electrical items, second-hand, and fancy goods, he told me to go and wait on the shop step for the arrival of a special gift for me. After an entire hour standing on the step, my imagination ran wild about what could be coming. Then a man drew up alongside me in his car. He wound down his window and asked if he had the correct address. "Yes," I replied excited, "this is the address," stretching my neck to try and see what was inside the car, but could see nothing.

"Well, do you like it?" my Dad piped up behind me. I couldn't believe it. Dad was pointing at the car! My very own shiny black Ford Popular had arrived. I was just about old enough to drive it. No one we knew had a car at 17 years of age. Dad had already booked driving lessons for me at the most expensive school of motoring. When I didn't pass my driving test the first time, he just booked me in for another set of lessons, and I passed.

My older sisters often reminded me how I was in the spoiled category, yet I knew he was good to them too. After I got married, Dad put down a substantial deposit on a brand new dormer bungalow for us, because neither he nor my Mom could tolerate seeing us living in the tatty damp manse owned by the church where Chris was pastoring. The little terrace manse was in School Street, Golborne; an old shabby neglected coal mining village in the North. The manse was one of rows and rows of houses that had been built especially for mining families. The steps up to the front door made it difficult every day to get the baby's pram in and out of the house. We had been warned to be particularly careful, as the previous Pastor's wife had tripped going down the steps with her baby's pram. The pram had fallen from top to bottom – with the baby in it!

The tiny terrace manse had no bathroom and only an outside toilet. We kept our tin bath hung up in the yard. We would fill it with buckets and bathe beside a coal fire. We would then drag the bath to the back door and tip the water down the yard. It was all too much for Mom to see when she came to visit, hence the deposit on a brand new bungalow.

We had been in our newly furnished dormer bungalow in Millingford Avenue, with its smell of brand new fitted carpet, for only nine months, when a missionary call came, quite out of the blue, to take the gospel to cave-dwelling - gypsies in Spain. I couldn't help but ponder if the call may have felt exciting if we had still been in the house with a tin bath! As it was, I felt numb.

With the "HOUSE FOR SALE" sign now deleted and replaced with even bigger letters displaying "SOLD" … it was my daily reminder of a very different life to come. So I thought I should begin to work hard every day on the fact that I was going to be a missionary, so would never live in a house again.

Early one morning our neighbours, friends, and church members arrived to buy everything in our home, carrying away furniture, wedding gifts, and all our other possessions, which included my precious piano I'd pampered and polished since I was twelve years old. Our home stood as bare as when we had moved in. We hadn't expected the bungalow to sell so soon, and especially not before the birth of our second baby. But to save losing the contract, we had to go along with it, even though I was seven months pregnant.

Calvin, our firstborn, was three years old. He looked up at me smiling, as he watched his bed, desk, and his new little birthday tricycle, happily scooped up and disappear down the road – believing us when we said it was all for Jesus. I sat on a remaining chair to rest after a weary day of selling and looked around an echoing room, which hours before had displayed my admired home-making skills.

I started to wonder if this was what faith may be: no home at seven-months pregnant, no church, no denomination, no piano, no anything. All our belongings now fitted in the boot of a car. As we drove away, with my baby kicking away inside me, the story of Lot's wife came to mind, as I gave a backward glance at the fluffy white curtains I had so painstakingly chosen, still hanging at each front window of the bungalow. I knew life would never be the same.

--oOo--

Now here, in this sad, forlorn mission-field, where electricity is rare, and where driving a vehicle is like being on a fairground ride, my lifelong burning desire to always be in God's will – no matter what it meant – or whatever the cost, is draining away. It feels sad to discover I am not who I thought I was.

But when we had set off from England to be missionaries, I was convinced I had well prepared and conditioned myself for living in difficult circumstances. I thought I had quite accepted that everything was going to be acutely different than in my modern, comfortable home, now being enjoyed by another. I thought I had fully come to terms with the fact that missionaries didn't possess much. But obviously, I mustn't have thought that God's will could be something quite as backward and dirty as this.

I crave to be back in England more than anything I have ever craved in my life, and would gladly trade pearl rings, gold watches, and all the fancy outfits, to be back in civilisation. I never knew that home sickness was a real physical hurt. I am already longing for family, friends, our church; to play my piano; to talk to someone over a telephone, or just to hear my own language. I can see how a missionary couple need to be deeply in love, and to be able to get on with each other, and enjoy each other's company, to exist in a lonely deserted mission-field. I feel some relief that at least Chris and I do have all that going for us, as there is certainly no one else around. It is so empty, so unconnected, so lonely.

We don't even know how to begin to be missionaries. There isn't a person to greet us with a welcoming smile, a reassuring handshake, or a God bless.

In the unaccustomed heat of our tiny new home, an ancient twelve-foot-long caravan, I agonize over Chris's offer to head back home, wondering if he would really like to soldier on, but can't ask him as I'm afraid of the reply.

I remember how exciting God's will was for us at one time, when we were enjoying the popularity of being "Kris & Kristine – The Sunshine Evangelists" – loved and admired by churches throughout our denomination. Although I was a shy and timid evangelist's wife, to Chris's relief, I always managed to overcome it as we walked towards the rostrum, Chris squeezing my hand to reassure me. I hated attention, but my big full-size gleaming red accordion helped me feel hidden somewhat, and we sang our hearts out. Chris played a guitar and sang tenor, and I alto. Chris's preaching was always well received. My part in our conventions was being the children's evangelist. How I loved children, and always felt full of confidence when doing anything involving children. We received invitations right across England, until Chris accepted the pastorate of the church in Golborne on the discovery I was expecting Calvin, our first child.

In my own familiar surroundings in England, I knew how to cope with my timidity, but in these primitive, undiscovered villages, where everyone stares at us as if extraterrestrial beings have landed, I freeze with fear and loathe being so noticeable.

I had never imagined that there were people whose lives only revolved around water. It seems to be a worshipped substance. It is collected only by the female population from a street tap or a well. Young women, little girls, and old ladies bent with age, fill a big heavy stone pot then carry it underneath their arm, or on top of their head. I am pleased that we have sons not daughters! I know I will never be able to do it as I am certain their heads seem flatter than mine. The task of the little peasant boys seems no easier. They pick snails from the scrubland then squat to sell them. We can't believe that there are human beings who put slimy bugs in their mouth, and ones that have been collected from scrubland. How can I ever fit in here?

The atmosphere is one of oppression, and even though the people seem to keep cheerful, there is a downcast expression in their eyes. They seem awkward whenever they see us, even turn away, and we are unable to understand why.

We need to park the caravan somewhere, and spot a big clump of palm trees which is inviting shade in a hot barren landscape. We make our own track to them over holes and ruts, the caravan wobbling from side to side, and we hear everything crashing around inside it. Chris, in his usual way, is trying hard to amuse us, but is catching on that it is a losing battle. The caravan has no sink or toilet, so Chris puts up our little tent to house the portable toilet, and a bowl to wash ourselves. We will need to go to the street tap for water to be able to use them.

We spot a rusty sign, and can just make out letters spelling 'Mojacar' which seems a strange word, but being already bored in this 'exciting location,' we decide to go to see what Mojacar is. We go through long dry riverbeds, and up and down ditches feeling like milkshakes and another sign indicates that this Mojacar is up a mountain. All I can see as we drive along with dust flying up everywhere, passing one ruin after another, with aged peasants clothed in black sitting outside them, is the prettiness of England and what a pity how we had never realized it. I can hardly believe that we are in a place on the planet where time has stood still, and how mules and water are all these people have in life.

Until now, I had thought that faith and God's will was something thrilling and exciting! Like miracles! Waiting on God! Believing for something impossible! Feelings of expectation! But it seems that this is my first lesson that it may not be.

We follow the sign to Mojacar. The climb is a steep and twisting one, on a narrow rutted dirt track just wide enough to fit a donkey and cart, of which there are more than a few. The track is thick with donkey dirt and the wheels and the underneath of our vehicle will never quite be the same. The smell is a ghastly mix of raw sewage and donkey dirt. The track goes around and around, and more donkeys join the line. We don't know if the peasants are staring at us in disgust or amazement. We are a novelty to them, just as all the wrinkly olive-faces are to us. Big old rickety carts with stone water pots and straw piled high join a painfully slow line. The straw is piled so high we can't quite figure how it stays put.

The peasants' heads almost twist off as they gaze back at us following along. The huge cart wheels wobble as if to lose their balance and topple over at every sharp curve.

The slow drive is a painful one coming from a country where people have things to do, and we see how *patience* would need to be the main fruit of the spirit here for any missionary. Cars are not suitable and I could see us needing to swap it for a mule – if we were going to stay that was.

At each curve we keep getting a glimpse of a stretch of gleaming white going across the very peak of a barren mountain. Then, as if a mystery is unfolding, our climb comes to a sudden stop, and we see that the stretch of white is ancient residences pressed into the cliff edge. They look more like rubble and must be risky places to live in. We have arrived to the very first hustle and bustle we have seen. The women are not only washing clothes by hand, but are standing up to their thighs in water to do it! They are crushed into two long narrow trenches all slapping down garments onto slabs.

The whole focus of life is water and is the reason for a cluster of ruins on top of a mountain – to be near the well. Dozens of female eyes are fixed on us as if we have dropped from space, or as if perturbed at having been discovered. The same oppression hangs in the air.

Chris gets out of the car to get water and women point at our plastic containers. Chris soon realizes, as grumbling gets louder, that he is the only man around. I watch him from the car manoeuvring around fly ridden donkey dirt, donkeys' rear-ends and wagging tails, to try and get near enough to the spouts gushing out water. The donkeys have priority over the trenches and these peasant women aren't pleased at them being disturbed. My eyes are streaming from such blinding light, the likes of which I have never experienced, and I can only squint. I have discovered I am allergic to heat and bright sunlight, and as I've never owned a pair of sunglasses in my life, I wonder where I will get some in this time warp before we can leave.

I pity these poor women, with tired lined faces, and such leathery skin, each of them dressed in an identical thick black dress and black headscarf in such intense heat. They slap down garments mercilessly onto worn slabs of solid stone, rubbing and rinsing, rubbing and rinsing. All the dresses float back and forth over the water which is building up more and more froth swirling around them as they wash. I wonder why they don't tuck the dresses up instead of battling with them. They keep glancing over at me, and I know their chit chat is about me sitting inside the car watching them. It makes me feel like a queen sitting in her carriage smiling at her common subjects, yet being a reassuring distance away from them. I study such unusually tall higgledy-piggledy houses dotted around the well, and am baffled at why anyone would bother to paint broken crumbling bricks brilliant white. I am so overwhelmed at the hard lives of these women, who carry heavy wet clothes in heavy containers, over lumpy tracks filled with animal dirt, goats and chickens, into their houses of dust and rubble.

Chris is relieved to get back into the car knowing he has made a mistake and caused serious displeasure and disruption. I am taken aback at the pathetic amount of water he has collected, after such a long drive up a mountain following donkeys to get it. Until I can get out of here, I have to cook, flush, and wash with it, and my supply of disposable nappies is all but gone. Also, it will have to be me who gets our supply of water, after seeing how men aren't allowed at a women's washing well. But I shudder at any remote possibility of standing in trenches alongside these women to wash clothes. I'd rather wear dirty ones. If there was one thing I did have back home in unappreciated jolly old England, it was plenty of clean, fresh hot or cold water at the mere touch of a tap.

Although Chris is still trying to entertain us, it is obvious that it was one thing to dream about caves and gypsies in a soft cosy bed in a sparkling new bungalow in England, but another thing in reality. We both realize we have ruined our lives. Even knowing what a huge disappointment and embarrassment we will be to our families and church, and what failures we will be to a denomination which said they couldn't send us – probably making them feel justified – none of it is enough to stop us wanting to get our little English boys out of this smelly backward place as quickly as we can.

We stand outside the caravan feeling abandoned and bewildered and have to accept what utter failures we truly are. It is my very first experience of self pity and the awful pain of homesickness. Chris puts up a washing line for me between the clumps of palm trees, then unfolds and positions our table and chairs – a reminder of a church we had loved and now lost – being their farewell gift to us.

We watch the biggest fiery sun we have ever seen begin to drop behind a dark mountain and we realize how the sun means absolutely nothing. I wonder if we had been going to stay, if behind one of the mountains is where we would have found gypsies or caves. We knew nothing whatsoever about gypsies. We had neither met nor known any. We didn't know if gypsies in caves even existed at all! We had arrived here on just one clue. A dream! A dream Chris had had back home in England!

Chris had awoken startled at five o'clock one morning while it was still dark. He sat bolt upright in bed and repeated a word "QUAVAS. QUAVAS. QUAVAS." He started to tell me how he'd been dreaming about himself in a cave with a dark, wrinkled, gypsy-looking man, yet only one word had been said throughout the dream, "QUAVAS."

I laughed saying, "the word just means music Chris. It is a musical note. QUAVERS." But for once, Chris didn't feel like joking, and didn't agree it was a musical note. The dream had gripped him and he couldn't go back to sleep.

For days and days he wouldn't give up trying to figure out what the word could mean. Eventually he wondered if it could be a Spanish word. The reason being, because he had been having special missionary prayer meetings at the church for various countries, one of them being Spain. He was convinced that someone in our congregation was going to get called to be a missionary, and in particular a girl named Marylyn. Chris felt she was the perfect missionary type just because she was so old fashioned for her young age and had her hair in the missionary type bun Chris seemed to associate with missionaries. But as the weeks and missionary prayer meetings passed, Marylyn didn't respond to any missionary appeals, no matter how much Chris 'nudged.' We were the only ones left praying about missionaries and Spain. But we didn't know a word of Spanish and certainly didn't know anyone Spanish to check if the word was a Spanish one. We lived in a small mining town of traditional old fashioned Northerners. There were no foreigners.

One day, Chris had an idea to go and buy a Spanish/English dictionary. He could hardly wait for the shops to open one morning. But much to his disappointment he still couldn't find any connection to a Spanish word. Only knowing how the word had been pronounced in the dream meant him searching for hours and hours through the dictionary, insisting the word had to have something to do with Spain, while I still kept going on about a musical note.

Then one day, I heard Chris shout… "I've found it! I've found it! It WAS a Spanish word Christine, and it begins with the letter C not the letter Q. The word is CUEVAS (pronounced quavas) and it isn't QUAVERS like you said, and the word means CAVES…the very thing I dreamt about!" We were flabbergasted. But Chris wouldn't even let it rest there. He went to buy a map of Europe to see if there was such a place anywhere on it called Cuevas. To our amazement our eyes were fixed on the word CUEVAS, on Spain's southern tip across the water from Morocco.

"It's a place called CUEVAS," Chris said, "and that's where we're going to." We stood together in silence gazing down at the map spread out on the table. "That's the place where we have been called to work for the Lord, Christine, and that's where we will find gypsies living in caves." My heart sank at the sound of CAVES, MOROCCO, GYPSIES, as I looked around my brand new home.

Chris immediately started writing a letter to our denomination about the whole thing, and to request their backing. We were totally dedicated to our denomination. Our entire lives and our family's lives revolved around it. Chris's Dad, as well as being a pastor, was also a well respected and well known convention speaker throughout our denomination. He had also been the closest of friends with the founders of it, like John Nelson Parr. Chris's brother was a pastor also. And as well as being a businessman, my Dad was a pastor, as were other members in my family.

Chris and I had even met at our denominational Annual Conference, when it was held at Middleton Towers, Morecambe. We thought it funny as my name was Christine Middleton. The Annual General Conference every spring was the biggest and most exciting event on our calendar, where thousands and thousands gathered. It was where all Christian girls hoped to meet Mr Right. One May, in 1962, I did!

As my friends and I walked around the chalets that year, we saw a big sign hanging from one chalet door. The huge gaudy painted letters said, 'CHRISTOPHER SMITH – LEAD GUITARIST AT FLEETWOOD FULL GOSPEL CHURCH.' In the West Midlands where I lived, and in our family, showing off, or boasting, was something unheard of. But it was also something quite unspiritual. It was also perceived as only what Americans did. So on seeing the sign, we all said, "What a big-head!" even though we were intrigued by who it could be. A few days later a young man, with the biggest greased hair quiff ever, resembling Elvis Presley, and wearing shocking pink socks, started to show interest in me. I couldn't help but be startled by his bold confident manner, and his immaculate, but unusual appearance. His pink socks matched a shocking pink shirt, and tie, which was outrageous at a Ministers conference. He started to boast to me, "My Dad's a pastor."

I answered, "Oh, my Dad's a pastor too."

Then he added, "We have a telephone."

I answered, "Oh, we have a telephone too."

Then he said, "My name's Chris, what's yours?"

I said, "Oh, my name is Chris too."

Then he said, "I play the lead music at our Church."

I answered, "Oh, I do too."

At this, he gave up, and said "Well, if you can't beat them, join them," and asked me for a date.

Later, my friends and I could hardly believe that it was the 'big-headed' lead guitarist I was having a date with. All around his chalet were hanging several brand new suits in unique daring new styles, each with a brightly coloured matching shirt, socks, tie – not to mention all the 'Winkle Picker' shoes lined up. He told us that he worked at Burton's Tailors in Blackpool, where image was important, and that he had dyed the shirts and socks himself to get the look he wanted.

His dashing good looks, his personality and especially his confidence impressed me, as I had always wondered what it must be like not to be a shy person. But his accent also took me by surprise. My friends and I had only heard the type of accent on T.V. We had started to watch a brand new programme called 'Coronation Street', and were fascinated at the intriguing accents we had never heard the likes of. I asked Chris to let me tape him speaking so that all of my friends and family could hear that I had a boyfriend who spoke just like the people off 'Coronation Street'. We all sat around one evening listening to the tape, giggling because I had met someone who actually spoke just like them.

--oOo--

Our denomination was proud of Chris, their youngest minister, just like they had been proud of his Dad, who was also their youngest minister in his day. There had even been five ministers taking part in my wedding ceremony.

So when a reply arrived, from our beloved denomination, to Chris's request about support for our new calling, we were absolutely astonished by it. The letter read, "We are all very moved by your unique and unusual call to gypsies and caves in Spain. However, owing to financial issues in the missions department, we are unable to send you."

We were baffled. We had been called to be missionaries but couldn't go! The feelings of confusion lasted for a long time. But Chris eventually thought of something which was of great comfort. His explanation was… "Christine, at least God knows we would have gone had it been possible. It was an obedience test, and we passed it." We went on our normal way in the church, but with the added benefit that the congregation admired us even more after having passed an obedience test. They knew we would have left all and gone to Spain had it been possible. I was staying in my house!

A while later, my Bible reading was in Hebrews chapter 11. I noticed how the list of people in it did rare things – and it was called faith. Even though I had read this chapter many times before, I felt enlightened somewhat. I somehow felt we could still be going to Spain. Yet I couldn't conceive how going to some unknown place all alone without any backing could be remotely possible. It seemed a ridiculous thought.

So I was determined that Chris wouldn't know how Hebrews 11 had affected me. I had kept it from him for long enough and could continue to do so. If we were being required by the Lord to do such a thing, I was determined that we wouldn't be doing it on any new insight of mine.

One day when Chris came home he said, "Christine, please sit down as I want to tell you something and it's very important." As soon as he said it my heart sank. He continued, "I have been thinking, that maybe we should still consider going to Spain, just trusting in the Lord. Would you be willing, or at least pray about it?"

--oOo--

Now we are here in this filthy part of the world, 'in faith,' whatever faith means to me now, feeling abandoned in the middle of nowhere, it is extinguishing any desires to live up to what I thought I was.

We grab candles as without warning the caravan is suddenly engulfed by inky blackness. Out there somewhere there is a place called Cuevas, but it can stay there, as all I can think of is the preparation for the massive wearisome journey back home on all those strange unwelcoming roads again, and how I will make such a journey without any disposable nappies. However, my green, busy, civilized and well-lit England at the end of it all will be worth it – even with our reputations in tatters. We know we will always bear the name *failures*, and will never be held up in esteem or admiration, or be listened to on any subject whatsoever, ever again. That's the way it would be and we knew it. That would be our particular lifelong burden to bear, and nothing less than lifelong it will be.

Outside our caravan, an orchestra of high pitched weird noises fills the silence. I am hoping and praying that whatever is making such sounds won't want to make our acquaintance tonight. I had only ever heard such whistling, hooting, and screeching noises on cowboy films on T.V. back home. They sounded cosy noises while cuddled up to a sweetheart on a couch. We had always thought of deserts as romantic with starry-lit skies, not dark, noisy, and suddenly freezing cold in a flash. The three of us squash up as close together as is possible, and around the tiny caravan table we begin to read the Bible under flickering candlelight, Calvin always eager to join in with a Bible reading. He is still brimming with joy over our new addition to the family sleeping peacefully in his carry cot; Wesley Adam, his three-month-old chubby baby brother, who arrived on October twenty-eighth 1970. These are the only members in our congregation now just the four of us. There aren't any hymns, choruses, or testimonies, like we had been used to, to stimulate any desire to pray impressive prayers or stir up feelings of spirituality.

My heart is breaking over the awful decision we have made to go home and what an awful embarrassment we will be to mine and Chris's Moms, who are held in such high esteem throughout a lengthy history of good names within our denomination.

Although our Moms were dreading us moving so far away, they had been so proud about their 'babies' being the first missionaries in the family, and they had done their fair share of testifying and boasting about it. I feel sorry for them. It will send shockwaves when we arrive back on their doorstep, let alone them having to find us somewhere to live. Selling our home and possessions, and people having special meetings and events for months to load up the caravan with food, had been for a life-long calling, like all missionaries, not for a month! That's why our Moms had been so broken-hearted when we left. We had been leaving them for good.

As we begin to pray, my tears are for myself and our Moms, but are mixed with twinges of joy for our two little boys going back to live in England, with aunties, friends, cousins and grandmas. We start by asking God to forgive us for being such utter failures, feeling like the children of

Israel. "How often they rebelled against Him, and grieved Him in the desert" (Psalm 78:40).

We then have the nerve to ask Him to help and bless us with our long journey back home, in a caravan so old it had already started deteriorating on the way down.

We begin to thank the Lord for Salvation and my thoughts go to the lonely route He must have walked when He came to earth and how it was far worse leaving the beauty of heaven, than us leaving the green and pleasant land of England. How He chose to come humbly as a baby, His cot being an animal's feeding trough. How His solitary journey with a lack of physical comforts, led to a painful death on a roughly hacked out tree.

I am suddenly aware of how getting to know the Lord, must mean having some understanding of the suffering of the One we follow. "Though being a son… He learned obedience by the things He suffered" (Hebrews 5:8).

My tears are changing. They aren't for self any more.

"For we do not have a high priest who cannot sympathise with our weaknesses" (Hebrews 4:15).

My tears are now tears of gratitude, my heart breaking out of repentance. Being severed for good from my country, relatives, and denomination, has seemed to pale in comparison with more of an understanding of His detachment from a sinless environment.

My tears have now turned into tears of submission. I even feel privileged because of something the Apostle Paul said. "We are fellow heirs with Christ, if indeed we suffer with Him" (Romans 8:17).

I have already learned something in this wild and barren silent wilderness, and am sure there is more I need to learn yet.

I don't need to ask Chris if he really meant it when he said he would take me home. He can sense we're not going anywhere.

The Lord is preparing me to walk alone. "For even Christ did not please himself…" (Romans 15:3).

It could take faith… to walk all alone.

"Even so, faith, if it has no works, it is dead (useless), being alone." (James 2:17).

2

It Could Take Faith...

to die to self

Our every move is being monitored. Two Civil Guards impeccably dressed in dark green uniforms, with shiny black bullfighter type hats, each with a machine gun, stand alongside their motorcycles from morning until night, chain smoking and jotting down our every going and coming in a notebook. I can't help but think what a boring job watching us! Why us?

I am making a true effort every day I awake to blank out England and its conveniences and unrealized beauty. But we had overlooked the most serious and precious thing we had left behind – freedom! The presence of the Guards hits home that we are now in a dictatorship. At least there is one thing we have in common with these peasants – none of us are a free people. Freedom is a thing of our past. Timidity will be a way of life for me here. The Guards' highly visible machine guns, so insolently displayed across their shoulders, aren't to keep people safe after all. They are a warning. We realize that the gloomy atmosphere, regardless of sunshine every day, is one of an oppressed people, and the expressions are ones of hopelessness. We have arrived to reach for the Lord, a race living in fear.

Guards or no guards, I have no option but to find a shop. Our little hoard of tinned and packet foods stored underneath the caravan bed-boxes by loving and concerned parents and friends, will run out. We haven't seen one single shop here let alone a plate glass window. I have absolutely no idea where to start. I recall the lovely English pastime of browsing and window shopping. But I crave the glimpse of a shop no matter how odd. I drive past our personally assigned Civil Guards, and like robots, their hands go straight to their machine guns. As if they are about to be attacked by little old me and my dictionary! Their steely look is one of intimidation. It is all so unbelievably backward. However, my dictionary and I will begin this life of faith by some action, which for me will be to search out shops, while Chris stays with the boys. I know no Spanish, or how I will pronounce a word even when I've looked it up.

Chris is surprised when I eventually arrive back at the caravan empty handed. I explain how troubling it is that we are in a place where there is nothing to buy because there are no shops. It is obvious how simple these peasants live, maybe growing all their produce, but surely no one can grow everything they need. If they can and do, I know we are in trouble. I am dearly hoping that the Lord doesn't want us to keep a cow or be farmers as well as missionaries.

A certain group seem well catered for to keep their sanity here. Ancient wrinkly-faced men who all dress the same: black trousers, hand-knitted tank top, black felt beret, crush into tiny scruffy bars which expel a pungent smell of coffee and brandy. They shout to be heard above the other, waving their arms furiously letting off steam. But such demonstrations of bravado only takes place in dark and dingy bars.

I can't yet resign myself to the fact that there are no shops as I was certain that all females everywhere in the whole wide world possess the urge to shop. There are plenty of cobblers' huts, where cobblers work away on the most worn shoes.

I decide on a plan. I will look for any female who is carrying anything at all, in the hope she may have obtained it from a shop.

I spot a woman who has emerged from a thick dark curtain hanging at a doorway and can see she has something inside a cotton bag. I go through the curtain, but can't focus due to going into such darkness from such blinding sunlight. All I hear is a woman shouting at me, "Que? Que?" (What? What?). It is because I have walked into her home. I rush out, not even knowing how to properly apologize to her. Another woman emerges from yet another curtain, and I gingerly try once more, and yes, I have found my local shop, even if it is only a porch. The porch has bucket upon bucket of dry bits the likes of which I've never seen. None of it looks fit for human consumption. All the unidentifiable grains may as well be bits of grit to me. I point to a bucket in the hope that the grey stuff could be sugar. A peasant lady, so painfully bony and ancient, in a thick black dress, and black headscarf pulled low covering most of her lined dark face, is sitting on a tiny low stool with the buckets circled around her. When I point at the bucket she grabs the scoop, lifts it up towards me, and without looking up to see me smiling at her, just keeps holding out the scoop. When there is no response, because

I don't know what to do with the stuff being offered to me on a scoop, she irritably tosses the stuff back into the bucket, and continues her statue-like position of gazing at the floor.

I feel as if I am insulting these people when I smile now we know what the oppression is about. They are a people with no rights. There is also a serious lack of motivation. Everything is done in such slow motion, as if nothing is worthwhile, or as if trying to fill the hours of a day. It is painful to watch. This will be a frustrating way of life for me, the way I have to do everything as if it is the last thing I will get done on my daily list. I am sure my brain will seize. Even young men stand or slouch around aimlessly staring at anything and everything, in a place of sheer nothingness. I am the something new and different to stare at, which I find extremely uncomfortable. I feel like an alien, while to me – they are the aliens of a bygone age.

I decide to wait inside the bucket shop to note what happens when someone is served and where I am going wrong. The ritual becomes clear. A customer points; the old lady scoops up; the customer holds out a bag, which has to be right at the point of the scoop; the old lady tips. I am going wrong because I don't have a bag. Their white embroidered cotton bags take me right back to when I was ten years old. According to school rules, my Mom had to make me a similar cotton bag for PT to take my plimsolls to school. My dear Mom was anything but a seamstress and had done her best, but I was so embarrassed taking that bag to school every week but didn't want to hurt Mom's feelings.

The frail lady who serves makes no effort to help whatsoever. One mistake and the goods are irritably dropped back into the bucket until another finger points. I never thought paper or bags could be something precious, and I can't wait to get back to the caravan to begin my collection.

As I go from one curtain to another making mistake after mistake of entering homes instead of shops, but at least having learned how to apologize for it, I look for clues to help me memorize what 'shop' sells what. I jot down any identifying marks as I have found a few 'porch shops' which sell a bit of this and a bit of that. My list reads: curtain with bit of thread at side/monkey nuts, curtain with ripped hem/rice, curtain with hole/grey sugar, curtain too short/lumpy salt, curtain in two pieces – don't know what it is in that bucket yet. Then it dawns on me that I have completed a new task alone, and a surge of hope arises that I may not be as useless as I thought I was after all. I just wish I could be more fascinated with such a backward way of life, or perhaps see it as quaint. But I could never be fascinated by this kind of quaint. It is a quaint that smells bad. A quaint that requires too much time and work for the most basic of tasks. A quaint with no choice of anything good to eat. We long for a real English meal of meat with gravy, and roasted potatoes.

I have no clue as how to prepare any of the dry boring bits I carry back to the caravan, which resemble what I gave to my budgie, but it's eat or starve. I keep trying not to dwell on our friendly Northern chip shop back home in Golborne. But at times I can almost feel my nose tickling from the salt and vinegar as the lady shook it over our steaming hot battered fish and chips. She would eventually hand Chris and me the vinegar bottle because we always kept asking her to put a bit more on.

My search for shops, while my every single move is studied by guards, peasants, and children, rewards me one day with a bread shop. Although it is still behind a curtain, it is obviously a place of more importance than a bucket shop because it has a counter top, with someone standing behind it ready to serve. It is so refreshing and functions with interest, even respect. Whatever is lacking in real food here, bread certainly isn't, and is the shop selling something that at last has a good smell to it. Yet people only whisper in the bread shop, which is strange as everyone shouts so much here. It reminds me of a library back home, where everything had to be quiet. The bread is handled as if it is something sacred or even a newborn baby. The atmosphere is funeral-like.

The bread lady is very old, very spindly, very frail, with a very leathery face. She is impeccably dressed, still all in black, but in a thin crisp well pressed cotton dress, with a dainty white lacy collar, and a finely knit black cardigan. A piece of black lace is pinned flat on her head. A sudden change to a sour face on seeing me ruins the whole sweet crisp clean effect she portrayed. When my turn comes, after ages on my feet waiting, because she chats in length to every lady who comes in – she shrugs her shoulders at me, and does a sign with her hands indicating 'sorry, no bread left.' Then she glares at me as if intimating what a nerve I have to have entered her bread shop at all! As I walk out confused and disappointed, I see her already getting loaves for the lady on the way in. So thinking there is a misunderstanding, I turn around and go back inside and stand waiting as they chat at length again. This time I ask for 'pan' (bread) thinking I may have been refused because I pointed instead of using the word for bread. But this time, she doesn't just shake her head, she totally ignores me, and leaves me in no doubt that I am not welcome.

I return to the caravan worried, because if I don't know

what to do with all the other bits everyone calls 'buena comida' (good food), at least I do know what to do with bread – eat it. We are all so sick of dry crisp breads from England, and are also longing for some butter. My Mom always calls it 'best butter', no matter what brand. It is her way of differentiating it from margarine, which she says is only fit for baking with.

On my next trip for bread, I try to show the dear soul how desperate I am, almost pleading. I feel relieved as she promptly disappears through the curtain to the back where she and a helper transfer the sticks of bread from ovens to long tables. I am pleased she has realized that I can't give up that easily. As she went through the back I got a glimpse of the rows of yummy steaming bread laid out on long tables. In England I had only eaten sliced bread, so I am desperate to try bread that looks so different, and smells utterly irresistible, as well as being the only tasty looking nourishment in this place. But after being gone for ages, she returns empty handed yet again, appearing more irritated than before that I am still waiting. She shakes her head signalling there is no bread. I plead, indicating that even one stick will be plenty. But she marches from behind her counter 'tut tutting' at me, and I can hardly believe how she then starts to 'shoo' me right out through the curtain with her bony hands and starts hissssssing at me – "sssssssss." This is the sound everyone uses to scare off a stray cat or dog, of which there are many. I am back in the street breadless.

It is going to be a time-consuming routine, as we have to have bread, and it is the only place we have seen any. I have started to wonder if there will ever be time to be missionaries and to do what we have come to do, with the hours it takes just to get through a day. It is a boring and tiresome routine.

Yet, there is something likeable about these people, and the look in their eyes when they see us seems an apologetic one. I think the ever present armed guard on every street corner is doing a lot to curb the friendliness from women who I am sure seem to have a desire to want to speak to me. But every time they show signs of it, a steely glance from the guards is enough. I want to put down some roots and try and accept this new life of faith, but can't see how it can ever be possible if everyone is so afraid of us. I find some comfort in reading about the people of faith again in Hebrews. Faith to them was not to regard any country as their home. They didn't want roots anywhere so as never to feel settled in any place, as theirs was to be 'a better place.'

Having learned that we have arrived in a place that had been under Moorish rule for eight centuries, we feel its lingering strict regime may have something to do with not accepting foreigners of such different dress, lifestyle, or religion. But we have also learned something else. Much to our utter surprise, we have discovered that we are the very first ones to arrive in this remote, undeveloped, backward location with the Gospel! This has helped us understand why we are seen as such a threat after years and years of an unchanged way of life. We are the very first missionaries and we reason that suspicion and fear is to be expected and things could take time. It is a place where no one has ever been allowed to own a Bible, let alone read one – and we have brought dozens of them.

How I desire to be accepted like the other women who enter the bread shop. They are so pleasant to each other. Their weary, worn faces – owing to years of carrying water and scrubbing clothes – in addition to fear and persecution – melt into smiles as they draw comfort from everyone else in the same boat. They behave like one big family, and I hope that one day they can feel as relaxed with me. When they enter the shop the bread lady shuffles into the back in her tiny frayed black slippers, and returns with piping hot sticks of bread for them. She then tenderly places the bread into their home-sewn bags, the bread handled as if it is some sacred substance. Her tiny frail face is so sweet when she smiles, but it isn't sweet whenever she sees me. I keep returning to our Palm Tree caravan residence empty handed, and "Give us this day our daily bread" has taken on a whole new meaning.

Chris is busy doing his part as a missionary, discovering the area, and we both hope that I am sufficiently safe to be left with Wesley and Calvin in the early morning hours at the caravan while he goes to explore, and to see if he can locate such a place called Cuevas or gypsies.

On one particular morning I step out of the caravan while Chris is gone, always dreading what could pop up next in this archaic place, and I have to be seeing a mirage! I know it's one because I have seen this kind of thing on films. When anyone is in a sauna of a desert and begins to crave water or whatever – the 'whatever' they crave suddenly appears before them. But before they allow themselves to believe that the 'whatever' is real, they reach out to touch it – only to find that there is nothing there at all. It was just a mirage! So – I drop to my knees to touch my 'mirage' before allowing myself to believe it is real, just hoping this slow backward way of life hasn't driven me mad already. But no! I am not mad – yet, and it is not a mirage. It is real! It trickles through my fingers like gold dust and means more than diamonds to me. To my amazement, in this relentless scorching dry desert, where the sun never fails to blaze day after day to torment us, and in a place where it hasn't rained for years, I have a proper little stream flowing right outside the caravan door! The ground is so hard and cracked, the water hardly penetrates it. I run to grab every item of clothing we possess, hoping the stream won't disappear as fast as it has appeared. Then every morning I step over the bodies of a snoozing family on the caravan floor to get outside as fast as I can to see if my 'mirage' is still there. Then, being too on edge to go back to sleep, I have to wash everything we own in case the sun dries up my 'mirage' that day. The washing is on the line before the family have even roused. It is my very own private stream, and I can hardly believe that I have been rescued from having to stand in line with the women in the Mojacar well. Another little surge of hope arises that things may work out for me here after all – or that the Lord may be having pity on me.

Chris is pleased seeing my joy about something, but is also preoccupied, certain he's discovered gypsies, and is anxious for us to go and meet them. There is a sudden, loud knock on the caravan door and we nearly jump out of our skin and I almost choke on a cup of tea. Chris opens the door to a loud and friendly, "Hola. Soy Francisco. Quién es Usted?" (Hello. I'm Francisco. Who are you?). I peep through the net curtain to see a very smart and distinguished looking man with jet black thick curly hair, smoking a huge cigar, and wearing a proper pressed shirt, and proper pressed trousers, which is all in sharp contrast to anything here. He certainly stands out as being someone important.

Chris is studying Spanish from books, but all I know is 'lo siento,' (sorry) 'pan' (bread), or 'buena comida,' so I just watch Francisco and Chris chatting. There seems to be some problem and when Chris realizes later how I haven't understood even one thing he and Francisco had been talking about, he strongly advises I make study of the language a priority. I know he's right. But there is so much to do, yet in a place where there is absolutely nothing to do!

Anyway, Francisco had informed Chris that the Palm Trees we had chosen as home belong to him. It's amusing and the first thing we had really found to have a good laugh about. It felt good to be laughing about something. If there was one thing Chris had always done, it was make me laugh. It had been another of his characteristics that had attracted me about him – but making me laugh is something he has found hard going of late. We never imagined that a clump of scruffy wild Palm Trees in a vast and empty ugly space could belong to anyone other than God. But neither was it God's stream. That is Francisco's too, and just an escape of irrigation from his vegetable field somewhere around.

He has given us permission to stay at the Palm Trees for a while, but made it clear that we should buy some land from him. He had explained he owned all the land as far as the eye could see, and that if we bought some we could stay under his Palm Trees while we built something on the land to live in. So, Francisco is a landowner, which explains a lot. But Chris and I think it hilarious. Why would he think that anyone in their right mind would want to own some of his salty, ugly, barren mosquito-ridden land, in the middle of nowhere?

Chris was hoping Francisco had understood when he explained to him that we hadn't come to buy land anywhere, or to build anything, and that we had come to live in Cuevas, to preach the Gospel, and distribute Bibles. It was too difficult to explain to Francisco the reason we were going to live in Cuevas, which was just as well. At the mere mention of the word Cuevas – he gave a look of disgust, and laughed and held his nose until he got back into his fancy French car chuckling to himself. However, it just felt good to see a nice car, and someone wearing somewhat normal clothes.

And – I'd had a visitor! Right here in the middle of all the emptiness, someone had actually come and knocked on our door like at a real home. We'd had contact with someone in our outer space, and someone who wasn't afraid to speak with us or to be seen with us, and without that look of hopelessness. It felt refreshing. I am determined that if Francisco comes again I will welcome our guest with a nice pot of English tea. If there was one thing I had made certain to bring from England, it was loads of comforting tea and a teapot – not only for myself – but because I had always enjoyed being hospitable, and had hoped I would be able to be so on the mission-field too.

--oOo--

With our crumpled map, we make the decision to find Cuevas, and hopefully gypsies and caves, much too aware that we may have come all this way to discover that neither existed. Then we would have to confess to our family, and the Lord, that we had got it all wrong!

We have already discovered Mojacar, the Moorish mountain top village with the ancient washing well that I have thankfully got out of needing. We have opened a Post Office box at Garrucha, the tiny, poor, smelly fishing port. We have also been to Palomares, a place full of tomato plantations, huge outdoor bread ovens, and acres of corn; a startling sight to someone like me who had never had a second thought of how corn got into its tin.

Then there is Vera, a most dreary place and our first sight of an absolute abundance of nuns. They scuttle around Vera's tiny, narrow, scorching hot streets in ballooning black habits that nearly touch wall to wall. The villagers walk backwards in respect, and bow to let them pass, and behave as if they have seen gods. The nuns carry lovely woven baskets overflowing with colourful produce that stand out in such a place of lack. I want to interrupt their rush to ask where they have got it all from, but lack both the courage and the language.

In Vera, there is a huge mountain with a stone image of Christ standing on its pinnacle, arms outstretched over the tiny village. At 12 noon it looks like a spontaneous game of 'Simon Says,' as church bells ring out while the system is affirmed over loud speakers in a drab monotonous voice. Everything goes dead. Everyone stands motionless, as the state dictates life over loud speakers. Then, as if people have been 'wound up' movement begins. We try to avoid the times when it happens. But as ugly, dishevelled and depressing as Vera is, it must be of importance as it is the place with the bank and the school. The school resembles a prison with its massive iron gates, rather than somewhere for children to learn. I shudder at the thought of the day Calvin has to start school, because of the warning we had from George and Marlene, two dear older missionaries we had met on our way down to our missionary location. As soon as they knew we were going to put our children in the local school, they were horrified. They made it very clear how "cruel and unkind" it would be to do such a thing. They said how we should never allow our children to attend a Police State school in a dictatorship regime, and especially in the dark primitive villages where we would be the first missionaries. They explained how they had been forced to withdraw their son, even from a city school, to be sent back to England for schooling because of the immense, intolerable difficulties he had encountered. How it had inhibited any chance of learning, and had made him desperately unhappy. They explained how the classes chant and do rituals most of the day and how their intense disapproval of any alternative way of life can be too hard on a child. I hate Vera because it reminds me of the day Calvin will have to face such a trial. Even so, Chris and I have decided, that whatever it takes, that our children won't be brought up by others in England, and that we will stay together, as a family. My heart needs to be here, not where my 'treasures' would be, "For where your treasure is, there will your heart be also" (Matthew 6:21).

Suddenly, on our way to finding Cuevas we spot exactly what we are out looking for: Gypsies! At least we assume they are, because they are at the side of the road cooking in the open air. A large untidy woman is standing under the shade of a ragged cloth strung between four canes. She is lost in concentration as she hovers over a big battered cooking pot boiling over twigs which keep arriving via the hands of naked children. Her plump dark round face pours with perspiration as she tosses weird looking 'grass' into the bubbling pot.

For the first time I see clothes other than black ones stretched out tightly over big prickly cacti drying in the sun, and I am grateful for such a good idea. Mangy, skinny, bug-ridden dogs scratch and snooze under rickety old chairs for shade. They open an eye to inspect us, but are thankfully too hot to budge.

I am shocked on seeing mothers continue to breastfeed their babies without any intention of covering up on seeing us arrive. Some mothers have one arm around a suckling baby, while the other arm functions on a chore that anyone else would need both arms to do. Some mothers are naked from the waist up because they are suckling two babies at the same time and I am embarrassed at the sight of it all. Toddlers run to and fro to feed as the impulse takes them. I don't know how Chris will be able to cope on seeing all this nudity right before him, while he has to stutter out his very first Gospel sermon in a new language! Men-folk carry on regardless, doing a seemingly worthless job of plaiting canes, while naked children run around with nothing to do, other than gather scraps of wood for the cooking, or plague the dogs. There is no discipline, and the children are followed here, there, and everywhere, being spoon fed. Grandmas crochet and knit, and it is easy to see that the shapes underneath the cloths draped over their laps, are tiny babies being protected from the sun.

I can see Chris ready with the biggest Bible he owns under his arm preparing to announce the reason we are here, with words he has practised and practised.

The only thing I had ever heard about gypsies was that they stole children, so I am hoping and praying, that if they are gypsies, that they won't want ours because of their pale skin and blonde hair. So we decide to leave them inside the car while I stay close by. I have to admit, that whatever the cook is cooking, it smells powerful and rather appetising, and I long for somebody to teach me what to do with all the funny foreign food here – even if it does only look fit for parrots. I am panicking at the thought they may ask us to join in their meal. I desperately want to fit in and like everything, but I am still heaving at everything I try, and wouldn't want to offend them. Some of the things going into the pot look like lumps of skin which turn my thoughts to doctors and if there are any in this place if ever any of us get ill.

I position my camera so that friends and family can get a glimpse of this primitive lifestyle, which sickens me as I suddenly realize how similar it is to my own now. But something obstructs my view. A large rough hand is over the camera lens, and a loud gruff voice shouts close to my ear, "NO! NO! NO PERMITIDO!" (No! No! No photographs allowed!). I force a smile to the big hairy-chested man without a shirt on that I understand. But I am disappointed that if they hate cameras our friends won't see any photographs. I am baffled how they are against photographs yet allow their women to have bosoms uncovered in the presence of foreigners. As I am putting the camera inside the car, I realize the mistake I have made by opening the car door. The man discovers Calvin and Wesley and there are shrieks of delight as everyone rushes over to see them. The vehicle is surrounded while I try to keep my eyes focused on two blonde heads through the cluster of dark ones, as dozens of hands go out to tussle their hair and stroke their skin, my heart pounding not knowing what to expect.

"WE HAVE COME HERE TO PREACH TO YOU GYPSIES," Chris pipes up trying to speak over the noise and to distract from the fuss over our lads. I just hope he is right addressing them as gypsies!

The cook was the only person who hadn't shown any interest in our visit, but she starts to strut from her cooking pot now – and makes for Chris. She presses her vegetable knife underneath his nose and proudly states, "WE GYPSIES ARE AS GOOD AS YOU ANY DAY – AND PROBABLY EVEN BETTER!"

Everyone present wholeheartedly agrees with a loud, "SI, SI" (Yes, Yes) and especially Chris.

We jump in the car speeding away from all the sudden anger, deciding we have done our evangelizing for one day, so to leave Cuevas for another.

That night Chris sits with his head in his hands, disappointed in himself, and asks God's forgiveness for his lack of tact, and asks Him for another chance.

The next evening, as the sun is dropping behind the mountains, Chris notices a group of travellers further down the track from our caravan and is convinced they are the same angry faces from the previous day and that they have come to find us. He rapidly hooks up the caravan and throws everything inside for off. So much for his 'another chance' prayer! In the haste, he doesn't have time to prepare properly and all the important wires and plugs are being dragged along rough ground behind the caravan as we speed off. Later, inside the caravan we sit surrounded by our smashed belongings, shaken and upset, longing for a friendly face, or some comforting words from someone, anyone.

Back home in England, before becoming missionaries, there was always someone to meet our need, either our church, our friends, or our denomination. Mostly it was our Dads. Chris's Dad had been our spiritual adviser on everything, whilst my Dad came to the rescue of our financial needs. Now, there is no one for us to turn to.

During the time we had been preparing to come to the mission-field, my Dad had a car accident, and his businesses were dissolved as he lay in hospital trying to remember our names. Chris's Father travelled down from Fleetwood to Wolverhampton to visit my Father in hospital, yet shortly after that visit to my Dad, he himself was taken ill with a new strain of Asian 'flu. To everyone's absolute horror, Stanley Smith, just one month after visiting my father in hospital, contracted complications from the 'flu and died suddenly!! I will never forget the impact. He had been such a powerful encouragement in my life. He must have sensed a lack of confidence in me because he always had a favourite sentence he said to me every time I was in his company, "You are as good as anybody love, and better than most." I can hear him now.

Our calling to a life of faith which had begun when our Dads had been comfortingly behind us, had never seemed so frightening on that bleak and blustery day at a grey deserted dismal English port. Boarding a boat in the New Year of January 1971 to a far off unknown corner without any organization behind us was a rare and scary thing to do. We didn't think for one moment that my father's accident, or Chris's father's death, had anything to do with our call to a life of faith. But during the boat-ride, Chris and I admitted to each other that it must have been at the back of our minds how both of our fathers had played some part in our courage to go to an undeveloped part, and that if things went wrong they were there to tell us what do to.

We were numb that day, as we stood leaning over the boat-rail being waved off by Chris's newly widowed mother, getting smaller and smaller as the boat sailed further away and as her turquoise silk scarf was waved faster and faster. My Mom was still caring for my Dad and couldn't be at the port to see us off. Chris and I were suddenly aware how we weren't only leaving home to begin a new missionary life without our denomination, but it hit us that it was without the crutches of our two faithful Dads.

Now as young missionaries, we are being forced to turn to the Lord in our mess and isolation and know we need to have as much trust in Him as we would have had in our Dads. We decide we should return to Francisco's palm trees, and not run away again. But on arrival I stare in shock at where my stream had flowed. Francisco has stopped irrigating.

The women standing in the water at Mojacar loom up before me. I am aware how our family is in need of clean clothes instead of always wearing mud-smeared ones, so I may as well accept the inevitable.

Chris comes dashing back to inform me that he may have located Cuevas, urging me to prepare the children so we can all go and see it. I suppose at last, we need to go and see the place responsible for turning our lives upside down. As we follow a road going out of Vera, the scenery starts to change considerably, even from where we are located, and a nasty odour gets worse until our throats hurt with it. The mountains on either side of the car starts to resemble another planet. They get higher, making weird shadows, and seem to loom over the vehicle. It feels claustrophobic. It doesn't help that we pass the spookiest of cemeteries, and see how their dead are buried in holes in walls – all stacked one on top of another, with photographs of the dead pinned to them.

The barrenness becomes even more so than where we are living. The mountains are changing to a creamy pale colour. They are pitted, and resemble the moon images.

I had hoped I had faced all the bombshells there were to face here by now, but this is the biggest disappointment and shock ever. Out of all the backward dirty ramshackle hovels, Cuevas is by far the most upsetting. There is nothing. It is nothing. It could never be anything. It is a dump of crumbling houses with a smell of raw sewage, and I cannot bear the thought of this ever being our children's home.

We are utterly stunned that a dream, and a call, and all our preparations and hardship for it, have been about such an insignificant place. "It's no wonder you needed a dream about it Chris," I manage to squeak out. "Because without one no one would ever find it, and no one would want to either." And how I was wishing we hadn't. I just want to get back to a caravan that suddenly feels like my cosy, fire-side retreat, and it is my first experience of being grateful for an old caravan underneath bug-ridden palm trees. However, Chris ignores all objections, and insists that we first check if there are any such things as caves. So with our fingers pinching our noses we go searching for caves while people stand motionless, jaws dropped, as we drive around.

"Look, Look." Chris suddenly shouts, "CAVES!" And there, dotted high up, low down, here, there, everywhere, and anywhere, in all of the odd shaped, creamy, moon-like pitted mountains surrounding Cuevas, there are CAVES – dozens upon dozens upon dozens. People are living in mere holes, like tombs in the cemetery, the only difference being – they aren't dead yet. We gaze in shocked silence, unable to take in such a primitive existence, making the well in Mojacar seem like a modern washerette. We stare at how people are living, puzzled that this Cuevas would even be on a map at all! Some caverns are so high up it is impossible to see how anyone could scramble up to them. Some of the cave entrances are whitened, while others have been left the same sandy colour as the mountain itself. Our eyes are glued to an unexciting fulfilment of a dream. "We've found them!" Chris shouts. "They DO exist," he says, "and it's exactly what my dream depicted: gypsies living in caves," his voice diminishing on realizing my disgust at any excitement in his voice. I loathe the word cave, gypsy, call, dream, or faith, and never want to hear them in our vocabulary ever again. I just want out. Yet, in seconds our car is swamped by dozens of beaming grubby children with not a pair of knickers or a pair of shoes in sight, but lots of dark uncombed matted hair, sticky noses, and masses of flies, the likes we would never have imagined possible. The car door handles are grabbed while we are urged to get out. I just want to escape, but dozens of grown ups begin to run from caves everywhere, dashing down from up the mountain through filthy tracks of wild dogs and chickens to get to us as if they have never ever seen another human being.

I am far too shocked to put on any typical missionary "Happy-to-be-here-and-make-your-acquaintance" look, a look I'd seen so many times on the faces of dedicated missionaries on missionary slides in meetings back home. I just feel hopeless and devastated knowing I am never going to be that typical missionary I'd admired all my life.

It is open the car doors or they will be pulled right off. Our children are then grabbed and shuffled between one child and another and from one cave to another, while we too are pulled in and out of cave after cave, each person urging us up various mountain tracks to see their cave as if it is better than the previous one, then looking intently at us waiting for a delighted reaction. My eyes don't adjust to the change of dark and light, so I can't make out anything in any cave, or who has our children.

I can't believe these are the first human beings happy to see us, and the only ones to have welcomed us, and who want to be with us, and they have to be cave people! Through the crowd I then get a glimpse of baby Wesley being splattered with kisses. A little girl picks up a lump of bread from a filthy floor, and I watch as she tenderly places the bread into Wesley's little fist, smiling at him with a face full of nurture and love. The bread goes straight to Wesley's mouth.

It is plain to see how children and animals use anywhere and everywhere for a toilet. They seem a neglected, unloved, and unwanted people, pushed to the outskirts of this tiny village to live in mere holes like moles. Calvin is laughing and so happy to see any children and is running around with them amongst chickens, goats, and dogs, which all exist together. Even though I loathe it, I can't help but see how overjoyed Calvin is to be with other children, hardly noticing the filth.

But it isn't a place for the faint-hearted and I know I am not brave enough. If this is a journey of faith, I do not possess the character, strength, courage, or even the spirituality, to be able to take one more step. If this is dying to self, I know that it will be far too painful a death for a person like me. Until this moment, I had hoped that I had already started to 'doze' a little, because of accepting I that am to wash in trenches of water. Now I realize I haven't even half closed one eye!

We arrive back at the caravan which seems like paradise, and I am crushed with the knowledge that I am just not missionary material at all, and never will be, knowing they are made of far better stuff. I am completely unable to comprehend why the Lord would send us. I ask the Lord to forgive me for being such a weakling, and gently remind Him how His speciality is changing people. But I am too painfully aware how change involves the too long a process of dying to self, and that dead people don't complain.

I recall preachers back home speaking boldly about being "BURIED with Christ," or "KILLING the flesh." As young people with a thirst for God, it had seemed exciting as we jotted it all down in our notebooks.

Yet deep down, I would really like to be more than a dry worthless seed. Deep down, I would really like for my little allotted grain to blossom into some fruit, no matter how small or insignificant, so that we can joyfully share the

Gospel with people who have never heard it as yet.

But I am too aware, that a seed can't be rushed, and that its burial has to come first. A seed has to be in its deep – dark – lonely – grave, all by itself – withering – shrinking – dying; struggling all alone to push itself up from its grave, and for a long time before any little shoot will show on top.

But surely with God's help I can allow myself to get buried. Yet, I am such a coward. I know how seeds get pressed, prodded, poked, and sometimes – even forgotten.

"God left him alone only to test him, that He might know all that was in his heart" (2 Chronicles 32:31).

But surely any seed, no matter how inferior the brand, will find some strength, with God's help, to eventually push up out of its shell, to get out from its deepest darkness into some light – if it has been down at rock bottom long enough that is.

The fact I have to face is that my single grain will remain just a single grain – unless it goes underground – inside mountains – inside caverns. Ugh.

"Truly, truly, I say to you, unless a grain of wheat falls into the earth and dies, it *REMAINS* alone, but if it dies, it bears much fruit" (John 12:24).

I can't understand why there couldn't be a quicker, easier, and more pleasant way to produce a bit of fruit.

It could take faith… to die to self.

3

It Could Take Faith...

to be brave

If only I could feel *some* disappointment. Day after day we arrive back from Cuevas weary, having again been unable to find any kind of room, cave, or anything to rent to begin our life and ministry there, and all I feel is relief, and guilt. We have tramped around for months while being stared at, pointed at, gazed at. I dislike being so visible, and had never experienced how uncomfortable it feels to be different from everyone else, and the one to stand out. However, because of it, I have experienced an entirely new emotion. Empathy!

Eventually, someone tells us to find Señor Borracho, the property man who will confirm that no one ever sells, rents, or moves, and that crumbling bricks are highly prized inheritances passed down through generations. We are also told how it would be unspeakable if anyone made things easy for the new 'predicador Protestante' (Protestant preacher) in any way, shape, or form, and that a person would be completely ostracized for it. This is confusing, as if no one sells, rents, or moves, why would there be a property man?

We locate the Señor Borracho property man, but he is not at all interested in us and not at all impressed on being woken up at six o'clock in the evening. He keeps rubbing his eyes to focus and keeps edging his way back towards the hovel which is home to him, and stating, "No soy borracho! No soy borracho!" (I am not El Borracho!). Chris apologizes that we have the wrong person and asks who it is we need to speak to. "Yo. Yo." (Me, me) he insists irritated, "Pero no soy Borracho" (but I am not the Borracho). This gets more and more complicated. We have been directed to 'El Borracho,' who says he is he, but says he isn't he! Every little thing here takes so much time – then from 2pm until 6pm an entire country sleeps – a 'siesta,' then even the 'every little thing' can't get done. Before Señor Borracho disappears, we just have time to blurt out to him that we want to rent a building – anything! But he snaps, "Imposible! Absolutamente imposible! No hay tal cosa aquí" (Impossible! Absolutely impossible! There is no such thing here) and with that rushes inside. I want to feel some disappointment every time it is re-affirmed that we are outsiders here, and that we will never be welcome in Cuevas, but all I feel is relief, and guilt for feeling relief. I did wonder though how we would explain it in our letters to people back home, how we have found the place called Cuevas but can't get into it. I have always carried a burden of not wanting to be the cause of disappointment to people, and especially to anyone who believes in us. I also feel it important to have a good name, and a good reputation.

Chris decides to reminisce a little. He decides to be of encouragement by referring to answers to prayer we'd had in the past, and how we shouldn't give up regarding

Cuevas. He reminds us of the predicament he'd had back home when preparing to come to the mission-field.

Chris had been concerned for sometime about how he would get the family down to our missionary location and where we would live once we arrived. There had been no one to help or advise us about anything, once our denomination knew we would still be going to the mission-field without them. They had informed us that they couldn't offer us any 'official help.' One evening Chris's scripture reading had been, "Whatsoever ye shall ask in my Name I will do it." The scripture seemed to press on him even though he had been brought up hearing it. He had felt to put his hand over the scripture and ask the Lord for a caravan, "Lord, give me a caravan to get my family to the mission-field and to live in, and please, give it to me tomorrow." That had been a Friday night and he was convinced a caravan would be on its way the next day Saturday.

When I saw Chris the next morning, Saturday, looking through the window waiting for our postman to arrive, thinking he may be bringing word of a caravan, I realized how seriously he thought he was going to get one. But there was no caravan from the postman.

I was impressed though, that it hadn't in the least put Chris off. I watched him prepare for his last district council meeting out of town. He said as they knew he was going to be a missionary, maybe someone would feel to give him a parting gift of a caravan. But he returned with, "No caravan Christine." Saturday came and went and no caravan.

The next day, Sunday, we were to travel to a little church in Bollington near Macclesfield where Chris had been invited to speak in the Sunday evening service. In the car, Chris was quiet and not my usual jovial spouse. Just before we arrived at the service, my hubby admitted to me that God must have said no to a caravan, even though he was certain he had felt some assurance for one when he'd prayed. "Christine" he said, "let's not tell anyone about my embarrassing unanswered prayer. Ministers need to encourage people to pray, not discourage them by telling them about any unanswered ones." We both agreed not to mention it to a soul, and Chris said he wouldn't even go near the subject of a caravan while preaching. And he didn't. He preached well, as always, and his excellent ability of mixing good teaching with humour always went down well, and he never as much as mentioned a caravan, or what he had prayed about.

After the service everyone shook our hand and wished us God speed on becoming missionaries saying their prayers would go with us. As we were about to get into our car, a man wanted to speak with us, and introduced himself as Mr Scott, but Chris almost had to persuade Mr Scott into telling us what he had on his mind. "Well," he stuttered, "I have a rather old and very tiny caravan." Then, almost in a whisper, and getting as close as he could to Chris's ear and as if asking a question, he said, "Actually I feel that God would have me give it to you?

Chris almost exploded with a, "Yes, Yes, He WOULD," which was embarrassing, but Mr Scott beamed. But even with Chris's outburst of excitement, I saw a hint of disappointment in his eyes, as if he could have kicked himself for not having mentioned the caravan in his sermon, or the story of his unanswered prayer.

When we got in the car for the journey home Chris felt bad. He said Mr Scott shouldn't have felt embarrassed about giving us an old caravan, but should have felt elated and encouraged that he'd had a part in obeying the Lord.

I started to wonder if it could take faith just to be honest.

On the way home however, Chris started to question. He was perturbed that with such a great answer to prayer, why God would only answer the first part of the prayer, "Give me a caravan," yet not answer the second part of the prayer, "And give it to me tomorrow." Chris made me laugh saying how it wouldn't have taken any extra power for the Lord to answer the entire prayer if he was going to answer it anyway. He kept going over in detail what had happened on the Friday night when he prayed, and what he had been doing at the time. I just kept saying how unimportant the details were and that the only thing that mattered was that we had the unexpected gift of a caravan from the Lord to get to the mission-field, and had something to live in when we arrived. I couldn't wait to pick it up to give it a good clean and pack it with goodies to take, but Chris was in his deep-in-thought mood. This always made me feel excluded and lonely, as nothing I said registered until he had sorted his thoughts. I called it Chris's 'other world' – and I wasn't in it.

"I've got it!" Chris said, "I know what happened. The Lord *did* give me the caravan the next day Christine! I remember the clock striking twelve midnight while I was praying so it was already Saturday. So the caravan *had* come the next day – Sunday!"

While we are both reminiscing about the caravan to comfort ourselves regarding Cuevas – the provision of the caravan having rescued us from living in the tent which now houses our toilet and sink – Francisco knocks on the window calling for us to go outside. We follow him around with Cuevas heavy on our mind. Francisco strolls around in his millionaire type strut, puffing his fat cigar and pointing out the piece of land he suggests yet again, we buy from him. He still won't accept that we are unable to do what he is requesting and that we are going to live in

49

Cuevas. He laughs again at the mention of the place, and tells us to forget such a ridiculous idea because no one will ever rent anything to us there; that we would never ever be accepted there anyway. He persists in pointing out the piece of land which he thinks would be ideal for us.

Because Francisco is allowing us to park under his palm trees, Chris doesn't want to seem impolite, so takes an interest in his land. We know though, that it is only a matter of time before we will have to move, once Francisco realizes that we aren't customers.

Chris goes into his other world, and I wonder what it is this time. But I don't have to wait long to find out. He blurts out, "Christine! I can't believe what it costs to buy land and to build something here."

Francisco is all eyes and ears on seeing Chris's explosion. I watch as Chris checks and re-checks facts and figures with Francisco, while Francisco keeps saying a loud "Si. Si. Claro" (Yes. Yes. Of course).

Chris quickly explains to me how the cost of buying land and constructing wouldn't even buy a bathroom in England. It seems we can buy land and build for around five or six hundred pounds which does seem ridiculous.

After the sale of our new house in England Dad had kindly wanted us to keep the deposit he had put down for us on the dormer bungalow even though we had only been in it for a few months. I will always remember Dad's words to us when we offered him back the six hundred pounds deposit after the sale of the bungalow. "No. No. You keep it," he said. "It will get you through your first few months of faith." Then chuckling as he added, "Then when the faith runs out I'll send you some more."

It's clear that the deposit from the sale of the bungalow is plenty for land and materials, but I am convinced this isn't what Dad had meant at all. But it's no use – Chris is already into the idea. "Christine, let's DO it," he says as Francisco's eyes dart between Chris and me as we discuss it, with me feeling a dampener because Francisco can see I don't look as excited as Chris, "Christine, let's buy Francisco's piece of land and build our own mission - station."

This is scary faith. I had seen Chris's house repairs! Everything he fixed back home needed fixing again. DIY wasn't one of his best points. So how could he know anything about bricks and mortar – and in a foreign land at that! So I can't understand why on earth I find myself joining in the handshakes all around.

But, we are the owners of three hundred and twenty square metres of salty, ugly barren land, with no roads, electricity, neighbours, or water, in the middle of utter darkness, all purchased with Dad's deposit. Nevertheless, it has made Chris suddenly feel like a missionary! "I saw it on missionary slides back home," he says, "Everybody had a mission station Christine. Now we'll have one too. We'll be REAL missionaries now won't we?" I was more than a bit doubtful that having a mission station would ever make me into any real missionary.

However, we walk around our piece of scrub-land in a daze. But I am alone again. Chris has gone to his other world.

Just as we thought, Francisco has given his permission to stay underneath his palms for as long as is necessary. 'Las Palmeras' (The Palms) is now officially home.

I feel a feeble little root descending, and a tiny brave urge to accept my new life and live like the rest have to here. So I start by preparing myself and the mountain of washing for a first visit to my 'washerette' in Mojacar. At least my little stream had delayed me going to the well, while I adjusted somewhat to the shock of what we had arrived to. We all pile into the car for our first journey to the only real activity here – a water trench – the family more excited about the adventure than me, as it isn't them who are going to get their feet wet. Chris is preoccupied again, about foundations, windows, and doors, but especially about a flat roof, which seems to be turning into his daily nightmare.

When we arrive at Mojacar, Chris places my buckets of washing at the trenches for me. I line up my shoes with all the others, trying to copy every procedure so as to fit in as best I can. But I am suddenly horrified at what I am going to do! A pale English woman is struggling between donkeys, their dirt, and odour, to stand thigh high in water just to have some clean clothes! Fear bubbles up as I realize I am not sufficiently settled in to mix like this. I'd heard of hand washing – but hand washing while standing in lather to do it is another story. Everything hits me at once. How they may chat to me. How I won't know how to answer back. How I am a novelty. How I am dressed differently. How I am the only woman not in black. I can't ever imagine being able to blend in that well ever, wearing such heavy garments in such sweltering heat. Chris feels as if he has walked into a female dressing room, and promptly disappears with our sons. We have noted how no men are remotely near any woman who is doing women's things, fearful of being seen as a sissy, and losing respect from all men.

I gingerly place my marble-white feet into the water which rises up to my thighs. As no one pulls up their dress it is ridiculously uncomfortable with wet clothing swaying all over the surface of the water, making a backward task doubly difficult.

With too vivid a picture of my automatic washing machine back home, now being taken for granted by someone else, I start to slap down my first nappy fiercely like them, onto worn-down slabs. I am shocked at the thought of just how many decades they must have been washing this way for solid slabs to be worn into a dip. The grey colour of what should be a white nappy compared to their brilliant white sheets, is an embarrassment.

It doesn't take long to see that it takes more than lining up a pair of shoes to fit in. These women are professionals. They are able to work up a frothy lather within seconds in cold water, while I can't get as much as a bubble. When I sprinkle English washing powder over a nappy, there are giggles, and I need to know where they have their washing powder pressed into solid round rubbing blocks. I feel stupid, and the last straw is when every female puts hands on hips in disbelief at the sight of mine and Chris's undergarments. What an impersonal way to wash clothes! I am entertainment for these women. It is probably the only fun and laughter they have had at these trenches in years. I just wish I wasn't it. Women are coming down from further up the mountain to the scene of all the laughter, and it's to see the foreign woman making a fool of herself. As I feel sharp stinging on my hands I can see it is blood because of rubbing on my flesh. Then as another hole appears in a precious irreplaceable nappy, through scraping it all wrong, I am wiping away tears, which makes my eyes smart from the washing powder on my hands. But I am desperate for them not to see I am crying. After all, this is normal life to these poor deprived women, and I don't want them to see that I am a soft mollycoddled English woman, or that they must have a hard life if it has made me cry, as there is nothing they can do to change things. I badly need to go home but Chris annoyingly hasn't returned.

I make a decision there and then that I will have to learn this fine art when I can be all by myself to practise it, which can only be in the dead of night. It will mean that Chris and the children will have to come with me as it would be unthinkable to drive along creepy dark riverbeds by myself, and we couldn't leave the children in the caravan alone.

So one inky black night at around midnight, we bed Wesley and Calvin down in the car and head out of our dark surroundings for Mojacar, our headlights the only lights piercing the darkness all the way. As the family snooze I get to work learning my new 'hobby.' I have the entire well all to myself, and there is just the sound of water from the tubes landing in the trenches. The water is soft and clean from the mountains.

At around 3am I am ready to leave, and wake up Chris who is snoozing in the car. I aim to hang out the dripping washing the next day as it is too eerie to do anything other. I feel some contentment that I have worked out a routine for my family's washing.

One night at around 3am we arrive back from the well. As usual, we first carry Wesley and Calvin from the car and take them into the caravan, then we go back to the car to empty the buckets of washing. But as we are returning to the car, without any noise or warning, two tall figures suddenly pounce out from behind the Palms and plonk themselves directly in front of us. They are Civil Guards with their machine guns pointing directly at us. They start to angrily ask Chris questions. I watch, frozen to the spot, as Chris fumbles nervously inside the glove compartment for our passports and visas. They want to know where we have been, and have a note pad to jot down the name of anyone we have been with, or any person we have spoken to. I stand trembling in a dripping wet dress, and freezing cold feet, scared to make any move at the sight of machine guns pointing at us, while Chris keeps trying to convince them that we have been quite alone all night and have seen no one. I am petrified and am thinking that we will be found full of bullets while our children will have slowly starved to death inside a caravan.

After deliberate painfully slow examination of our papers and without another word, the guards slink back into the darkness, just leaving us to work out if we are free to move. There is no sound of a motorbike to indicate if they have left.

I hate living this way. I yearn for a free, peaceful, protected homeland called England, which I would really know how to appreciate now. How I long to feel that sense of belonging again. So many times back home I'd heard preachers state all knowingly, "If a person is in God's will, or if a person is called somewhere, or is on an assignment for Him, a person is HAPPY and enjoying it!" Well, I am now in a position to disagree! We do feel called. We do feel in God's will. We do feel we are on some assignment for Him. Yet one is neither happy nor enjoying it. I know my denomination wouldn't be too impressed at how I have already changed from what I had once agreed with them on.

We are too nervous to light our candles in the caravan thinking it could be a sign to someone else of where we are. I am petrified as we grope around in utter blackness knowing we won't be able to trot out to the toilet tent throughout the night. I sob all night long as I caress baby Wesley's tiny soft hand, seriously doubting if I can ever be a brave enough soldier to be of much use for the real battles in God's army, knowing how soldiers are trained to suffer hunger, exist alone, take risks, put up with inconveniences and the unexpected.

"...Suffer hardship with me, as a good soldier of Christ Jesus" (2 Timothy 2:3).

But I don't like hardship. I don't like suffering.

How nice it must be, not to be weak or fainthearted.

I think about Esther who said, "If I perish, I perish," and what conviction, nerve, and courage she possessed to carry out her calling. Then Paul and Silas, who after having their clothes torn off in prison, and after having been beaten with sticks, sang hymns!

It could take faith... to be brave.

Paul the apostle was certainly the kind of soldier qualified to give advice. He was a soldier who could not only outrun footmen ("If you have run with footmen and they have tired you out, then how can you compete with horses?" Jeremiah 12:5) but he was one who could even rejoice during training! "We also exult (are happy) in tribulations, knowing that tribulation brings about perseverance; and perseverance, proven character, and proven character, *hope*. And *hope* does not disappoint..." (Romans 5:3, 5).

"Be strong, and let your heart take courage, all you who *hope* in the Lord." (Psalm 31:24)

One needs to be tougher – and one can only *hope* it will be so.

At long last, I am drifting off to sleep, but it is getting light, so now the baby is waking up!

It could take faith... to be brave.

4

It Could Take Faith…

to be a helpmate

As I scribble designs for our mission station, I keep peeping through the caravan window waiting to see the very first truck arrive with sand. The civil guards are now doing much more writing than smoking. Trucks arrive with gravel, cement, and massive boulders. The supplier tells Chris that the boulders are needed to fill in the foundations, then laughed as he asked Chris how any could be dug out without machinery?

However, the supplier is still proving to be helpful, giving Chris plenty of tips, but at times also frightening him, making him realize how little he knows about building. As if that is news! Chris is so pre-occupied about a flat roof. Nevertheless, I can't help but be proud. It is my husband, having a go at building his own mission house. I can hardly believe it. If only we had someone with whom to share this joy.

Chris resembles an ant alongside all the mountains of stuff keep piling up. All I see is Dad's money in the shape of grit and gravel.

We sit outside the caravan scribbling one design after another of how the building should look, while keeping glancing over at all the materials, commenting how cement can all be left uncovered here, rain being as rare as the sun in England.

One day, we look over at the massive piles of sand, gravel, cement, rocks, and boulders, and something hits us. What are we thinking? What have we done? How stupid can we be? How is Chris going to use up all this stuff? Even if he could it would take him years to do something as ridiculous as this alone in a foreign country with not one scrap of machinery. There are more tears and more prayers, and then Pepe comes to mind.

We had met a young and lanky exuberant Pepe only once, but one could never forget Pepe. On our journey down from England, we had passed through a place where a missionary couple were. How I admired them. They knew everything there was to know about being missionaries. I did so want to stay with them for a while, and learn more, knowing there was no one waiting at our destination to answer my many questions.

Calvin had taken an instant liking to Pepe. He was the missionaries' brand new nineteen-year-old convert, and they were over the moon about him. Pepe had already started to suffer persecution because of 'his change of religion' as his relatives called it, but it wasn't dampening his new experience one bit. His personality was like that of an overactive toddler. He was so elated about becoming a Christian, that he kept expressing how he now just had a desire to help any missionary anywhere, and even offered to help us. He asked where we would be located, and we mentioned Cuevas. He then told us how his wife was from Cuevas!

We left and journeyed on. We hadn't taken Pepe's offer of help seriously, as genuine as he seemed. The one thing the missionaries felt it was important for us to know right from the start was that 'Mañana' (tomorrow) never came.

However, from inside our caravan, while we are still fretting about building materials, the silence is disrupted by the sound of a spluttering motor-cycle engine. "Christine, its Pepe! He's come, even finding where we are." Not one person in the whole wide world knew where we had parked under the palm trees. But Pepe had scouted around until he'd found us. Pepe looks with glee at all the frightful piles of sand, gravel, cement, and boulders, and laughs about our concern. He says he has a few months to spare before his call up to the Navy and will help Chris build a mission house. Pepe is thrilled about his wages of twenty five pesetas an hour, plus his meals, and says his digs can be in the toilet tent. He says he will make the long motor-bike ride back home on Fridays to be with his wife and baby for weekends. We have a new friend! And Chris has a helper! Now there are five of us in our congregation.

Calvin is ecstatic, and he and Pepe behave like mischievous little boys, pulling faces, and just doing stupid things together. Calvin's endless hours alone, only having goats to watch, were becoming a cause for concern. A goatherd stands motionless leaning on a stick, staring in our direction all day. We are baffled how a human being can stand so still, for so long. I am grateful for Pepe's arrival more for Calvin's sake than Chris's, as there are no shops to relieve boredom with a puzzle or a toy, and no T.V., telephone, or comics. Wesley is too young yet to be a playmate for Calvin.

All of us walk over to the land together and we kneel down on it and pray. Pepe prays in Spanish, and Chris,

Calvin, and I pray in English. None of us have a clue what Pepe has said, or he us, but the Lord has sent somebody to be with us, and even someone who is not only interested in what we are doing, but someone who is really excited about it. Pepe is even a builder!

But then Pepe tells us some bad news when we show him drawings of what we want the structure to look like. He warns us that it must not resemble a church in any way, shape, or form. It is a terrible blow, as this was our purpose, and the most important thing to us. He explains how there are people in prison for far less, and we get to know some of the horrors about this province of Almeria we have arrived at.

We learn that although the Civil War had ended in 1939, that the cruelty continued. The province of Almeria had been Franco's greatest opposing province, so had been the most persecuted even after the war had ended. Massive arrests took place, and we get to know about the stone crosses on a hill near our land; simple village peasants gunned down for a mere suspicion. Thousands were rounded up and imprisoned, even shot. Franco's forces continued to punish people who had ever opposed him. We learn how those accused of political crimes, whether false or true, didn't get a hearing but were just lined up by a firing squad. Many ran for their lives to live as fugitives in caves. Franco gave them the name of 'Bandits'.

We find out from Pepe why we are being watched so closely every single day, and the danger we are in, and why the guards had interrogated us that night when we had returned from the well. Pepe tells us how that even now, a Civil Guard is not permitted to be a Guard in the same village as where any relative of theirs lives. The reason being that if any relative were involved in anything controversial, the guards may dither and lack the courage at the last minute to shoot their own flesh and blood!

Apparently, even until the late 1950s the very basic of foods were rationed and life was miserable and poor and people lacked bread. Poor Pepe thinks, twelve years later, that things have changed for the better!

With the building work about to kick off, we wonder how Chris and Pepe will ever be able to understand each other, because of the time it takes to have a conversation, searching through dictionaries, and drawing pictures. Yet begin they do, and with just five tools: a spirit level, a spade each, a hoe, and a 'funny black rubber bucket.'

I watch them hour after hour, day after day, struggling to get a spade into ground that hasn't seen moisture for years. It seems impossible. After long hot days of back breaking work, they eventually see a glimmer of hope of getting some foundations on the go. They faithfully toil until the foundations are three feet deep, and a square of one hundred and sixteen square metres. What a sight to behold – looking into what two slight men have done all alone with only a spade each. The foundations now have to be filled with the mountain of boulders – each boulder having to be picked up one by one and tossed into the trench, then all of them having to be concreted into place, and every bit of cement mixed by hand. I watch them stoop, lift, stagger, then drop. It looks as if such depth can never get filled in by two people. After one mountainous pile of boulders has been used up – along comes the laughing supplier with another pile for them to stagger with.

Fridays are horrible. On Fridays Pepe leaves early to go home. It feels empty again with his personality missing. He has so soon become a close friend. Even baby Wesley seems to be missing his daily bounce on Pepe's knee. Every

Monday morning, Calvin is always waiting patiently on the building site, jumping up and down as soon as he hears the sound of a spluttering bike in the distance – then runs to meet Pepe.

Mondays are favourite days – even for Chris, knowing it means the start of another week of staggering with boulders.

My daily entertainment is watching Chris and Pepe having 'discussions' over a brick or a frame. Then we find out some ridiculous news from Pepe, and some of the missionaries' 'tips' come to mind; people here exaggerate or boast. Pepe isn't a builder at all. He is just a self-taught plumber!

I can't believe how our lives are going to depend on each decision a plumber and a preacher make. I pray constantly that the Lord will give them wisdom, because a certain scripture has certainly come alive for me,

"Unless the Lord builds the house, they labour in vain who build it." (Psalm 127:1)

As Chris and Pepe get more and more worn out, and as they stumble back towards the caravan each evening over scorching ground, carrying the spirit-level and two spades, I can't help but cry at the sight of Chris hobbling, and how his hair now resembles that of a scarecrow, dry and sticking up like straw. Watching them build with such inadequate tools, and the agony it's causing them both is a dream turning to a nightmare for me. Even sunburn is something Chris isn't accustomed to, especially sleeping in a cramped caravan.

No matter how desperately I need every drop of precious water throughout a day, so as to get out of going up to Mojacar as much I possibly can, I always sacrifice some chore so that the men can wash. But more often than not, it ends up a cat-lick as I fail each day to be able to save enough water for two men. Then they both almost fall asleep over the food I have made. It is becoming a boring monotonous routine for us all.

I catch on quite by accident that Pepe isn't enjoying the food I make. Apart from being tired as he eats, he is also bored and disappointed with the meals. He reluctantly admits it when I keep pressing for an answer, and confesses it is totally void of interest or flavour. I feel so sorry for the way he has suffered in silence and admire such grace and good manners. While he has been working so hard he hasn't been looking forward to an enjoyable meal. I tell him that I am even more bored with the food than he, and we have a great evening of laughter talking about some of the terrible meals he's had to endure.

The problem had been that I had been combining what little I had left of English canned or dried food, with the local food which I hadn't known how to use. It must have been a terrible concoction for Pepe.

But I will always remember Pepe's look of shock when I was making mashed potato. He looked stunned on seeing white powder in the bottom of a bowl suddenly appear as a pile of fluffy white mashed potato when I poured boiling water over. It was the first time he had ever seen instant food. He insisted on an explanation knowing I hadn't peeled any potatoes. His same astonishment happened with a packet of dried soup. But his admiration for England's magical instant food ended once he had tasted it.

The next Monday when Pepe arrives he pulls out a long string of bright red sausages from his bag, and the smell of them is overwhelming. Pepe is baffled at our lack of enthusiasm, when the smell to him is so delightful that he keeps holding the sausages right up to his nose to breathe it in. We are puzzled how sausages can be such a fiery red colour, compared to the delicate pink of our sausages back in England. Fortunately, Pepe explains how these kinds of sausages need fresh air to dry out so as to bring out even more flavour, so he asks if he can string them up in our toilet tent! We tell him what a great idea, knowing none of us would probably wake up ever again if he had wanted them in our caravan.

When I visit the construction throughout the day with refreshment Chris says how Pepe's conversation for the entire day has only been about the sausages, and how he can't wait for supper-time, but not just for himself. He is excited that we will be able to try proper food at last. He expresses his sadness for the English, and how they have to tolerate such a poor diet of powdery food. Nothing can convince Pepe that we have delicious food back in England and he keeps on about how Spain has the best food in the entire world – even though he has never been anywhere else in his life. I just want him to tell me where this 'buena comida' happens to be. We had never realized how much food had really meant to Pepe, but on reflection, there isn't much else of interest here, apart from their offspring, who are little gods to everyone.

I go into our tent to use the portable toilet. As I am literally using it, I glance up at the sausages. There – hanging upside down, their tails hooked around the string are mice eating away poor Pepe's sausages, and I can't get up to get out. Even my screams don't perturb the mice one bit, and they just carry on nibbling away.

Pepe is crushed when I go and tell him the news. But the whole incident starts a new venture for me. Pepe wants to show me where to get the kind of things he would like to eat, and asks if I would follow his instructions on how to cook them. The Lord has sent me a chef! At last I am going to learn what to do with this funny looking stuff that has robbed me from the pleasure of cooking or eating, and maybe we will even get to know where to get some meat. How we are longing for meat.

Now Pepe's secret is out about not enjoying the food, there is no stopping him. Pepe is an extremely happy-go-lucky person anyway, and always on top of the world, but it had been nothing compared to the knowledge that he can choose his own food. He is ecstatic, and I wonder if I will go down as having been Pepe's first trial in his new Christian life.

Spanish men know nothing domestically, and would never be seen in a shop, just as they wouldn't be seen helping with their own babies. A man and a woman's work are clearly defined and no one crosses the line. Pepe explains how he will indicate to me what to buy, without him being seen as a shopper. He finds a tiny market square, right up a hill at the back of Garrucha where fruits and vegetables are displayed on tables. Teeny weenie bits of unidentifiable scraps of meat and red sausages are plastered in bluebottles. Pepe laughs when I comment on it and says, "Claro (of course). It is because we have sun in our country Cristina!" Nevertheless, I am thrilled when I find the same solid blocks of soap the women use at the washing well at only six pesetas each.

I am pleased how things are looking up. Even the bread woman has given in. One day at the bread shop I heard a lady whisper in her ear, "tiene niños." The lady who whispered it then left the shop in haste. The only thing I knew was that it had worked because I left with a loaf. Then after that, although I am still made to wait, I am not denied bread. I learn from Pepe that the lady had told the bread woman that we had children to feed, and because children are treasures, none are to be deprived of anything. Pepe also explains how bread is seen as sacred, and is the reason it is handled with such respect, and the reason they kiss it before they eat it. We hadn't realized we were coming to such a superstitious place. I am told why the bread lady had treated me badly. I am the wife of the 'predicador Protestante,' and she was being loyal to the system to make things difficult for us, in the hope we would return to our own country. Pepe also explains that it is only because we have small children that we have been safe here at all so far, because the 'system' doesn't want us here.

At last, I am learning how to prepare some food, but the strong smell of it all still makes me heave – especially 'pimientos.' I have always disliked green anything, even green clothes, but especially green food, that's why my Mom never put cabbage or peas anywhere near my dinner plate. These green 'pimientos' smell, but then Pepe tells me to buy something smelling worse – a little thing called 'ajo.' Pepe wants me to put loads of it with all his meals, and says I don't even need to cook it as he will eat it raw. He is in stitches on seeing me wearing a mask as I peel off the pink skin, and Chris calls me the 'Cisco kid.' We are just pleased that Pepe is sleeping in the open air after devouring this 'ajo' stuff because his breath knocks us backwards. I just hope that Chris doesn't take a liking to these little pink smelly things, or he'll be in the tent along with Pepe and the mice.

Pepe starts singing some songs and Calvin soon picks up on a favourite. It is a reason to get out my accordion for the first time, from under the caravan seat, to learn Spanish songs. Calvin's face beams whenever his favourite is sung, "Yo Tengo Un Amigo Que Me Ama, Su Nombre es Jesús"

(I have a friend who loves me, His Name is Jesus). I practise it while the men build. It's something a bit different to do than watch them lift a boulder, stagger with a boulder, drop a boulder, or to watch washing pile higher as I put off going to Mojacar more often than not.

Pepe arrives as usual one Monday morning, and comments how quickly his time has gone and how he has only two weeks left! We are shocked and can't believe it. Two weeks! Pepe is: our builder, our shopper, our missionary trainer, our Sunday school teacher, the chef, baby Wesley's 'knee bouncer,' our congregation, our chorus teacher, our friend, our adviser, our denomination – everything. Now he says he is leaving us! Pepe had even formally introduced us to an entire shanty street of gypsies. We'd had our very first evangelistic meeting there due to Pepe. I had played the accordion and taught them Calvin's favourite chorus, and Chris had preached. Chris thought he had been preaching in Spanish, so couldn't understand why Pepe had kept translating each sentence he said. So when they got back to the caravan, Chris asked Pepe why he had kept repeating what he had said when he had taught him Spanish. "No, No," Pepe said. "I haven't taught you Spanish Cristobal, you taught me English!" Chris thought Pepe had taught him Spanish, and Pepe thought Chris had taught him some English. They had formed a new language between them.

We had even been invited to a Gypsy wedding, a very private affair. The wedding went on for three long exhausting days, but we were allowed to go home each morning at 2am, but with a promise to return the next day to continue the celebrations. Pepe said it would offend if we did otherwise as an invitation meant an invitation. Each night I felt we would never hear properly again as they sang and clapped with such volume, while the women danced Flamenco in bright coloured home-made frilly dresses. The worst part was when I was suddenly pulled up from my chair by Luis, one of the guests. How I wished I had kept hold of baby Wesley, but it was too late, and Luis insisted I dance Flamenco with him. He was baffled by my objections. Back home in England, I wasn't even allowed to knit, have the television on, or even read a paper on a Sunday, let alone do twirls with a strange man. I kept trying to get back to my chair, and eventually Luis realized it was hopeless and let me go, much to my jealous husband's relief. But Luis told me he must teach me Flamenco one day, so that I could dance properly with him! The food is sweet and sickly, and is left out on tables day after day to carry on with the celebrations. I dread the children being ill as every female has to push food into all children's mouths, as if they will die of starvation if they don't. They follow toddlers around with dishes and spoons, shoving food into them.

A gypsy daughter getting married is the biggest event. The bride and groom have never even held hands prior to their wedding day, and have never been alone together, even to speak sweet nothings. We see courting couples chaperoned every second of every day and night, and who only speak to one another with an adult standing or sitting in between. A daughter would be left on the shelf – the most disgraceful embarrassment to a family – if she had ever been alone with any man, even for a second. We are told how no man would ever marry a girl who had not been chaperoned, and how a young lady is visibly protected until the day of her wedding. There is a commitment from mother, father, older sister or brother, and grandparents to take turns to chaperone.

It is explained to us how during a wedding reception, a bride goes through to a private room with her mother-in-law where a very personal test is performed on the bride. It is to prove to the groom's parents and relatives right there and then, that the bride is pure. Even though they already know that she is, it is still required to be proved publicly at her wedding. The groom's mother emerges from the room, everybody waiting for her appearance, then the entire room erupts with joy at the sight of a piece of cloth she holds up, at which all the men rip open their brand new wedding shirts, and everyone begins dancing, drinking, rejoicing.

We wonder if they will still welcome us when Pepe has left us, as we realize we may not get all the cultural aspects right when Pepe isn't around to whisper in our ear whenever we are putting our foot in it. Pepe apologizes profusely on seeing how distraught we are about him leaving, but confirms his call up date has come through and that he has no option. We somehow thought that it wouldn't really happen. Apart from missing him dreadfully, the building is nowhere near finished.

We feel we will cave in with sorrow as we watch Pepe's rickety little moped 'put put' out of sight for the very last time. How we will miss his fun and laughter, his mischief, his advice. Calvin is distraught.

With Pepe well and truly gone, I look up at the pieces of string still hanging from the tent-poles where the sausages had hung and sob. When Monday morning comes all of us automatically look towards the bend Pepe came around and we loathe the silence. It breaks Calvin's heart to sing the chorus. Pepe has left too vast a space.

I am now waiting for Chris to humbly admit defeat concerning the building, more than ready to understand when he does. I think this is one missionary's dream that can never come true. Even if there were machinery it would still be an arduous task for two men, but for one man without machinery, it is impossible.

I have never had so many conversations with the Lord, or cried, or prayed as much as I have here. I am either crying, praying, pining, squinting in intense sunlight, or scrubbing clothes on stones. I have always had a dread of ageing, and I fear I will look much older than my years down the line. All my moisture creams have now been used up.

Now here I am crying about something else as I watch my Chris walk over to the land, to work on it all alone. But as the tears are streaming down my cheeks, an incredible realization comes to me. *I* can be Chris's new helper! His new helper can be his own wife! By this time, I know as much as Chris and Pepe about building. I have eaten, lived, and breathed it from seeing the very first spade struggling to get into stony ground, and since seeing the very first lorry arrive with sand. I have been bored of watching the same mix of three spades of sand, one spade of dry cement, one spade of gravel, then placed into the 'funny black rubber bucket' for the helper to pull up to the roof on a piece of rope.

So, in between looking after the family and all the other things good moms do for their brood I start to help Chris finish the structure. He gives the orders, I carry them out.

We both begin to lose weight. There is no strength or time to make life family-like. Calvin is lonely and bored always playing around gravel and bricks, and watching goats, but the urge to complete spurs us on. So we force ourselves harder each day towards the exciting time to move in.

If watching two men build had been boring – boring was better, and rubbing clothes on concrete slabs a doddle.

I'd never ever thought that being a help-mate could be so painful, and that it could actually mean being a husband's work-mate. I am fed up of being filthy all day, smothered in grit, dirt, and cement; having sand and stones stuck between my toes and underneath my nails; my hair being glued to my head with sweat mixed with floating dry cement – and no bath!

A scripture in Genesis isn't much comfort, reading the reason why I was created. Until I'd read it – I'd been more than happy to mix cement.

Then the Lord God said, "It is not good for the man to be alone; I will make a helper suitable for *him*."(Genesis 2:18)

But I never want to be quite as suitable a helper as this ever again!

It could take faith… to be a help-mate.

5

It Could Take Faith…

to be grateful

The serious morbid voice coming over the airwaves from the BBC world service, from our little plastic turquoise radio, is unusually clear tonight. It is the hour we gather around to listen to our own language. But Chris is horrified. "They can't be serious," he blurts out in disbelief. "Don't they know what their ridiculous actions will do to us out here, buried in the deep, without anyone to help us? Christine, what are we going to do?" Well, I didn't know, so I couldn't tell him. Yet the announcement again was loud and clear, confirming the awful news that has so startled Chris.

"This is the BBC world service. There is no doubt now that there will be a serious postal strike in Britain, which could, unfortunately continue for some time."

Chris is shattered. "Christine, how will God meet our needs if the post can't arrive?" Well I'd never thought until he said that, that our only possibility of living a life of faith was down to a postman.

"Christine. We've used all of your Dad's money on bricks and mortar." As if I didn't know!

Dad's words echo in my ear, "Keep the deposit from the house, because you'll need it to get through your first few months of faith."

Although we'd never had any actual promises of financial support, friends and family had started to help. However, as Chris says, even if they feel constrained to send something, it will just be piling up with all the rest of the mail inside the post office in England.

Even so, Chris still goes faithfully to our P.O. Box No. 224 in Garrucha every day, just to return downcast and empty handed saying, "Just the holes in the bottom of the box love" – the holes being what are visible on the bottom of the box when it is empty. I feel sorry for him, knowing how concerned he is for his family.

"Christine" he says one day, "What if this walk of faith isn't going to work after all?"

Then our little butane gas-bottle fizzles out, so we find ourselves collecting sticks for a fire to cook on, from flea-ridden sand and a tick-laden mosquito-ridden wilderness, Calvin thinking it great fun. I never thought that because we had come to witness to gypsies that we would be surviving like they do – cooking in the open air. Perhaps they would accept us even more if they knew.

The third week into the strike and Chris decides to go to the bank in Vera to see if anybody may have wired an urgent gift. No one has, but a kind wide-eyed bank-man offers Chris a razor-blade for a shave.

Chris points out how everybody back home is probably thinking, that because we came here with Dad's money that we are O.K. He is right. Everybody did know that we had gone to the mission-field with a nice chunk of Dad's money.

Into the fourth week of the postal strike and Chris is still returning with the same tiresome sentence – "Just the holes in the bottom…"

Wesley is now on his very last box of baby milk and every bit of 'magic' food has gone, including the tins of milk I had brought over for tea. I had been brought up without any thought of being grateful for everyday basics. Now I am giving thanks when it's me who finds the chunkiest bit of wood to cook on. Looking back, I suppose I had never known much about a 'Sacrifice of Thanksgiving.'

Our denomination had told us – "We are unable to offer you any official help."

But having been sent to this neglected corner to bring the Gospel, I would like for it not to be anyway – to travel hours around mountains – to get to other missionaries to plead for their help whenever we are in trouble. I would see it as being no different from running to our Dads. I miss being in my denomination, and miss our Dads more, yet for the first time I crave for us to have the strength to look to the Lord without always expecting someone to be there to rescue us.

I can't believe it. What a time for Francisco to turn up! He is parking his fancy car and I have no milk or sugar. It will be too embarrassing to tell him why we have no beverage to offer, and no matter how impoverished a person is here, they always offer a caller something, even if only a few peanuts in shells, or a few round green smelly things they love called 'olivas.' "Oiga. Oiga. Escuchen," (Hey there, listen) Francisco shouts. He tells us how he has collected all the vegetables he needs from his patch, and that we can take whatever is left over. He points over to the same spot as where my stream water came from. This is something new, a need being met by someone other than our Dads or the postman, and someone who isn't even a Christian, and someone who has no idea of the mess we are in. Chris's eyes frantically meet mine as we both try to look calm, but wishing Francisco would hurry and leave, so that we can go and collect dinner.

I scout for carrots, onions, or celery, and all the familiar vegetables I know Chris would like in a soup. But all we can find are row upon row of oddly shaped solid green things resembling tiny cabbages but with pointed flowery shaped leaves. "I don't believe it," Chris says, "This is the only vegetable Francisco has planted, and we don't even know what they are." So, it has to be a vegetable soup with just one vegetable, if it is a vegetable that is.

When I submerge the weird unsavoury-looking things into a bowl of water to soak, I cringe. Umpteen earwigs rise to the surface. Chris decides to make some enquiries at a bar what the vegetable can be, and comes back to explain that they are alcachofas. We are none the wiser, but I proceed to cook them as directed, in a bucket on the campfire so my pans don't get ruined. Once boiled, we apparently have to pull the leaves through our teeth and what is left behind is the food. It seems a detestable and desperate way to eat, and is nothing less than rabbit food. I think Chris has misunderstood at the bar on how to cook and eat them, as it seems a lot of trouble, to wash, peel, and boil something, just to pull a leaf through teeth. I am convinced Pepe would never call this an eating experience, or 'proper' food.

After a never ending week of alcachofas, I try giving thanks, in case this is what is required before the diet can be changed.

But when the strike continues into its fifth week, I can't believe we are still giving thanks while gagging on alcachofas. Chris is still returning from the P.O. Box every single day to repeat the same tedious sentence of – "Just the holes in the bottom of the box love…" and I don't know why he even has to say it, as I can see that nothing in his hand he brings.

While Chris is over at the construction alone one day, the goatherd gives me a fright by signalling that I go over to him. Thinking he may be asking me for a glass of water, I still only take the dictionary. He indicates he needs an empty container and sends me back to the caravan for one. When I return with it he starts to milk a goat, and hands me back a container of warm frothy milk. I feel sick at seeing milk expressed from a goat, then the warm feel of it through the container. I had never heard of goats' milk. I didn't even know goats had milk, and my intention is to tip it away. Then I realize I have no alternative but to feed Wesley with it, and to use it in my tea – cringing at the thought of digesting bubbling goat's milk. The goatherd indicated to boil it, so I keep fanning it to get it to cool quickly so Wesley can have a feed. After the feed, I watch and wait to see if his tummy is going to object to a strange new fluid, every hour seeming like an agonising two. But thankfully, nothing happens.

The next day, the goatherd arrives and signals again. Wesley is now being reared on goats' milk. My Mom would have a fit.

We are in the sixth week of the postal strike. Chris is adamant that never again will we live on alcachofas or milk via a goat. "I'll be prepared for trials of faith next time," he says. As if every trial of faith is going to follow the same pattern! "I'm getting chickens, rabbits, and geese. We'll grow our own vegetables too Christine." I knew it! I knew from the start we would be farmers as well as missionaries.

It is the seventh week of the strike, and my eyes close at the sight of an alcachofa. It's hard for a human to give thanks for rabbit food and getting harder still.

It is difficult now to locate the BBC world service to see how the strike is progressing as the batteries are so low. We also don't have petrol to get to the Post Office, so Chris walks to it every day. The washing is now piled so high we have to start using it over. I know it will take weeks to get through washing it. I never ever thought I would actually be longing and craving to get to that awful well water and even be grateful for it, like everybody else has to be.

"It's over! It's over!" Chris suddenly shouts out one night, with my little turquoise plastic radio pressed right up against his ear. "I heard it, I heard it. I know I heard it. The strike has finished." But even though it is over, we know it will still be alcachofas and milk before any mail arrives from home, and we still don't really know if there will be anything even then, because of Dad's money. Chris is particularly pleased that the strike is over for another reason. He is convinced the goatherd has been using the milk as an excuse to get friendly with the foreign woman.

--oOo--

The post is normal again, convincing Chris even more that a postman is definitely the way God meets needs.

I make the decision that I will do the washing during the day like everyone else. The family is weary of the night-time routine anyway, and I too am grateful for any water anywhere. I am hoping my washing technique has improved, and at least I am not a pale English woman any more after being a helpmate. I also have the proper moulded soap blocks. I am ready.

I step into the trenches petrified, but when I get unexpected immediate nods of approval as I begin to scrub, the fear melts. The nods and kind smiles are ones that indicate, "This is what we do, and how we do it, and this foreign woman has bothered to get it right." I silently give thanks that I have grasped the technique. But I feel a bit of a fraud. I hadn't learned to rub clothes on concrete because of wanting to learn this particular facet of their culture, like they seem to think. It is just clean clothes we needed, and as I didn't want to be laughed at – learned it in secret. But I can't admit that to them, or even explain it in the language. So I will just have to revel in a little admiration.

If only our parents knew how we have come through a trial without their assistance. If only my sisters knew that I have been giving thanks for alcachofas. If only the Mission's Board of our denomination knew we hadn't needed that 'official help' they weren't going to give us anyway. If only Mom could see me, living in a caravan, and washing in a well.

As I stand in line with these women, learning more of the language, and slapping and rubbing clothes, working up as much frothy lather in cold water as quickly as they – with not one hole appearing in a nappy, I start to wonder if I could be one of those real missionaries after all.

But I am far happier about a new lesson I have learned. A lesson about God's will.

I had always thought God's will was something complicated. That it was something extremely difficult to unravel; something that had to be sought with fervour. We had been taught that anyone anxiously seeking God's will, were the most spiritual of people. We had always esteemed such ones. But I have learned God's will can be something quite simple as well as spiritual. It can be as simple and as spiritual as giving thanks. It is possible to be in God's will whenever I give thanks – for *something*.

"*IN* everything give thanks; for this is God's will for you in Christ Jesus". (1 Thessalonians 5:18)

Because I had not read that scripture with proper attention – I had always thought it meant that I should give thanks *FOR* whatever I was going through – no matter how awful!

I knew all the time that I hadn't really been grateful for alcachofa leaves to eat. It had seemed like lying to the Lord every time I was giving thanks for them.

I am so pleased. I am pleased because I won't need to give thanks ever again *for* some test or trial I am hating. From now on when I am going through something awful – I will be able to give thanks *IN* it – instead of *FOR* it!

I know it could still take faith to give thanks *IN* everything. But it certainly makes more sense, and will be easier, than giving thanks FOR everything.

During the alcachofa test there were things I could have been giving thanks for – IN the circumstance – DURING it, like a nice husband, and two lovely sons.

It could take faith… to be grateful.

It could take faith to find something to give thanks for during something 'awful', but the Lord has a good reason that we do it.

6

It Could Take Faith…
to resign to the unexpected

The day is getting closer – to move from underneath the palm trees. One thing is for certain, that living underneath palm trees has cured me of any notions of holidays or romance, the very things my friends and I used to dream about back in England whenever we saw palm trees in a holiday brochure. My screams must be heard in Vera whenever I run into the caravan, as hairy monsters of spiders and huge centipedes crawl out from their homes in the palm trees when I am hanging out washing. The day I told Mom and Dad I was going to become a missionary, they laughed thinking I was joking, knowing my utter trepidation of bugs, how I was reduced to helplessness at the sight of even the smallest spider. I will always remember Mom and Dad's expressions as it dawned on them that I wasn't joking about being a missionary.

Before Pepe had left us for good, he gave us clear instructions on where to get white paint to paint the mission station once the external blocks had been entirely coated in cement. Apparently, there is a good reason that every ruin is painted white. It is to reflect the sun, but is also to keep down insects, the latter interesting me most. The ugly grey blocks have all been coated in cement, and we can't wait to see it all sparkling white to give us the feeling it is ready for occupation. However, even though Pepe had told us where to buy the white paint, he had omitted to tell us the most important of details about it. Chris gets the paint from a lady's house in Vera. It is in rock form and they have to be submerged in big drums of water and stirred with long wooden sticks until the mixture turns into a paste.

But as soon as we toss the rocks into the water, there is loud hissing, then a cracking, then an explosion! When it all bubbles and jumps out like a witches brew we run for our lives. The heat from the drums is like fire, and it's impossible to get anywhere near the drums let alone stir the solution. We have no idea why paint would behave so ridiculously.

We have no option but to leave the mixture. A few days later the drums become cool at last and it can be stirred; the painting can begin. It all seems such a backward thing to do when we realize that an entire block structure all coated in cement will always need re-painting. As we paint the top of the building, with a brush fastened to a long pole, the mixture drops over us like rain. As the days go by, I am in absolute agony due to tiny holes which keep developing all over my hands, fingers, and toes. It feels as if I am being slowly burned alive with red hot match ends, or being eaten alive by something. The agony from the ulcer type holes is so intense I need medical attention. We go in search of a doctor suddenly realizing it won't be free like back home. So I have another thing to add to my mental list that I shouldn't have taken for granted in England.

Someone directs us to a little house opposite the port and a portly middle aged gentleman with a kind round face answers the door with a click of the heels. His head drops as if a King and Queen have arrived. He keeps his head bowed while his hand goes out in military-style to shake Chris's. With yet another click of the heels, he introduces himself. "Buenos días. Con mucho gusto. Yo soy Don Pedro. Estoy muy contento de conocerle a usted." (Good morning, I am Señor Pedro, and I am very pleased to meet you).

We are shown into his home and he introduces us to Concepción, his attractive wife. All the time the doctor is speaking to us, he lifts his head only occasionally, when his eyes briefly meet Chris's, but avoid mine. Then all his attention goes straight to Calvin and Wesley, when he is notably relaxed. It's as if they have known our children all their lives, or as if we have taken grandchildren to see grandparents, because of the fuss over them. Concepción disappears returning with dry biscuits and glasses of milk for them.

The doctor then starts to give us advice, gently, yet firmly advising to take great care to keep the children from the sun and flies. The doctor is confident and relaxed when his focus is on the children, but is notably shy, when dealing with us. This attention and attitude towards children, when in company, is so new to us, and so opposite to back home where children have to 'be seen and not heard' when in the company of adults.

The doctor asks, on seeing my wounds, why we would 'cal' the house without having covered ourselves properly. We don't understand what 'cal' is and it sounds comical because of Calvin, who is 'Cal' for short. The doctor is shocked that we didn't know we had been painting with pure lime! We had misused a dangerous liquid, never having seen or heard of lime for painting. Thanks Pepe! The doctor takes us into his tiny medical room, which is sparse and depressing. It is sad to see a doctor having to work with inadequate worn equipment in such dismal facilities. The doctor's traditional manners are intriguing, and his compassion even more so.

I leave the room resembling a mummy. Chris and I don't know what to do concerning payment, as it is obvious that even a doctor is as needy as everyone else here. But the doctor asks Chris if he would consider teaching his sixteen-year-old son, José María (Joseph Mary) some English in return. Chris happily agrees.

The doctor's attention goes to the children again, and he asks us with such concern in his eyes, why we would bring such delicate children from a place like England to live in such a wild place of heat and flies. Then his wife wants to know why we would risk our children's lives sleeping on a flood plain in a remote field, because a Spaniard wouldn't do such a thing to a child! "Well that's good news," Chris whispers to me flustered by it. Chris kindly assures them by telling them that we feel God has guided us and that there must be a reason why this particular piece of land was made available to us. They seem taken aback, yet satisfied with the answer. They are very religious people, and on hearing that we are here for God, they say that they will be of help in anyway they can. The doctor offers Chris any help he may need in translating sermons! He also makes it clear to call any time of night or day for any medical needs we have, without charge. I begin to wonder if Chris will have to admit soon how our needs can be met without a postman, and that a postman may not always be the only link to survive a life of faith.

We leave the doctor's house having made new friends, and people who absolutely adore our children.

After the completion of the lime job, which takes the biscuit for being the nastiest job of the entire project, we decide to take a drive to find some pebbles, stones, or something to make a sign to place outside to indicate the property's purpose. We find ourselves in 'Los Lobos,' where there is a riverbed full of slate from a slate mountain, and we fill the boot. Chris cements the slates and we paint on them 'Centro Cristiano' (Christian Centre). We even find the courage to position the sign boldly at the entrance. We are willing for the risk after having gone through so much heartache to build it.

With my fingers, toes, and arms, all still smothered in bandages, Chris and I stand well back to admire a gleaming white structure, the blinding sun rebounding off the whitewash, reminding me how I still need the sunglasses.

It's our little marvel. We hadn't had one piece of machinery. We had arrived to a strange new country. We'd had no one to turn to or talk to for any advice, except for one self-taught plumber and a laughing supplier. We didn't know the language or the culture. Above all, Chris had never been able to do DIY jobs without it being a disaster. But we did it! We just wish Pepe was standing here admiring it with us too, as Chris and I are in awe, gazing at our snowy white wonder.

The building isn't what one would call attractive, and only resembles what is called an old 'cortijo' (farmhouse), which is just a boring square, with a flat roof, the thing responsible for giving Chris so many sleepless nights. The inside is split into two, with a door in between to each part. For the family's half we designed a lounge, two bedrooms, a bathroom, and a kitchen. One half is our meeting hall, and will sit 40-50 people. The hall means everything to us, and is such a comfort, after not having been allowed to build the Centro in the shape of a church, and not having been able to get into Cuevas. At least having a meeting hall, we can see some form of ministry – the only reason we are here.

The day to move has arrived! I have so looked forward to this big day. Moving house in England was always such a big stressful event. I know because my Mom had moved twenty seven times! But I am more than ready for as much stress as I can get from moving. But after having taken down the bathroom tent, then having dragged the caravan to behind the 'Centro', the moving day is complete, and over so quickly.

My mind is on one thing, a bed, with a real mattress, which we obtained from a lady in Cuevas who sold beds from her house.

I have dreamed about the normal everyday activity of tossing sheets over a mattress to make a bed. It will be sheer joy to even walk towards a bed, instead of stepping over bodies on a caravan floor, and the never ending struggles to change the caravan seats into a bed, which collapsed most nights whenever we turned over.

All the things I won't need to do flood my mind all at once, but the very first thing on my new 'NOT to do list' will be NOT to wash in a trench again! I also know the first thing that will be on Chris's 'not to do' list. It will be not to dig a hole every day for the chemical toilet. Then there will be no more showering underneath a sprinkler off a watering can, and we will be able to clean our teeth under running water instead of using a cup and spitting over the ground. Now, my pots, pans and crockery, can pile up in a sink, like in a normal house, instead of standing under a cloth in a bowl in the tent, all of it plastered in flies.

Even though there isn't any water or electricity yet, just the very knowledge that there will be one day is more than enough for me to plan everything I am going to do once it arrives. I place my pots and pans inside a real kitchen cupboard, and put my now scratchy jaded towels in a blue tiled bathroom – which I tiled myself while being a helpmate.

So, we are settled in our little marvel. It is going dark and we have noticed that because bricks hold the heat, we won't be able to move around to do jobs for much longer, and especially once candles are burning. We rush around trying to get organised. We have had no idea as where to get any netting, so the windows will have to stay closed, which will increase the heat. It already feels like a steam room, the opposite of the caravan at night, so I think to place a bowl of water by each of our beds to be able to sponge ourselves down throughout the night.

We are hoping we are safe, as we have noticed how every building, whether shack or ruin, have thick iron bars on any opening or window, to enable occupants to sleep safely with windows open. But Pepe had never mentioned anything about iron bars.

At the feel of my body sinking into a mattress, I start to drift into a blissful sleep knowing that both Chris and I can turn or fidget as much as we want without worrying we are going to end up on the floor like in the caravan.

As we drift, it isn't long before we are jolted out of our blissfulness by a terrible din. The candles have burned out. In thick darkness there's panic trying to find the matches to see what is happening. It is horrific! The whole place is brimming. Crickets, beetles, lizards, grasshoppers, flying things, and there's even a snake and a mouse. It seems that behind every bathroom tile there is a noisy cricket trying to sing its way out. The bugs haven't moved into our home, it seems it is us who have moved into theirs. It is impossible to scare them back into their holes with a mere candle; darkness is daylight to them. So I feel I have to watch and march around with a candle all night long, crying, sweating, and praying for mercy.

When daylight eventually happens, I can hardly believe how normal everything looks, and how silent it is, yet I know there are hundreds of eyes watching and waiting in every crevice to plague us again.

Chris and I realize we were too anxious to move in. The place wasn't sufficiently finished off, making it an open invitation to the entire wilderness. So the lime never did do its job of keeping insects down after all.

Chris feels it a backward step to move back into the caravan. So each day becomes a race, filling in holes and gaps. But as soon as the sun starts to drop behind the mountain, my panic begins. I feel it will take me a lifetime to eliminate a wilderness of bugs. My heart misses a beat at the mere thought of ever having to get used to them being part of our family, an impossibility for me.

I try so hard each night to get to sleep before Chris, or at least at the same time, but Chris is annoyingly asleep as soon as his head touches the pillow. At his first snore, half apologising for it, another long tormented sweltering night of keeping watch has started for me.

I desperately need that escape route that the apostle Paul mentioned in 1 Corinthians 10:13, "He will not allow you to be tempted beyond what you are able, but will provide a way of escape." I feel I am in hell, because bugs are what hell would be for me.

"I've heard the water and electricity are going to be connected Christine," Chris says one day. My escape route has arrived!

I am experiencing such extreme contrasts of emotion – sorrow, joy, loving and hating. My life is certainly a big roller-coaster.

I stare at the tap, wanting to see the first drop come out, knowing it will mean the end of my Mojacar experience, my nightmare from the day we arrived. But I'd done it! It was all over. I feel the need to reminisce. I have learned to cook peculiar food, now even getting some enjoyment from some of it, mix cement, tile, and build. Now I feel challenged to live bug free. I am determined to make it possible to sleep without the fear of something crawling into our beds during the night. I will spend my life mixing plaster and bunging up holes, if that is what it takes to sleep without marching about or keeping one eye open. I have felt like the temple watchmen – the Levites – protecting the house of the Lord through the night, "…All the servants (watchmen)… who stand by night in the house of the Lord." (Psalm 134:1)

The water arrives and I can't wait to wash my hair under running water, wash some clothes in a sink, flush a chain, fill a kettle from a tap, but I run around not knowing which to do first. But it can't be true! The water coming through the tap smells and is salty! They have connected us to dirty salt water from the port. The first time I wash my hair, it is sticky, stiff like starch and stands on end, and smells. Our clothes are like cardboard. My cups of tea are yucky. We heave as we clean our teeth. But worse – baby Wesley's skin starts to peel due to salt remaining in the nappies. The rawness of his skin is so deep and intense he can't have a nappy on any more, and I can't find anything to heal the wounds. Chris says that the water pipes will corrode and that it has been a total waste of time installing any.

Chris goes to see the sand and gravel man about it. He laughs about us thinking we could use water from a tap except to flush or mop with. We have to order big drums and find a certain 'water-man', who delivers good water he collects from the mountains. For a price, Miguel fills up our drums each week from his lorry, and we have made another new friend.

It is all so disappointing and unexpected. How could we have been so naive? Here we are on an isolated plot of land, undeveloped and topped in salt, years behind the twentieth century, and in a desert where rain is a long awaited annual event, thinking we could have normal utilities. It is still a sad realization that the basic utilities an English home takes for granted, and ones we had been so looking forward to enjoying once again, would be the absolute of luxuries here.

I can hardly believe that after all the rush to get the place finished that I will still have to stand in a trench to rinse salt out of nappies, and I feel well and truly devastated, and also confused about the 'escape route' I was convinced had arrived.

Then the electricity is even less impressive. It had been installed by a young lad called Domingo (Sunday). Everyone seems to have a religious name, and even the name Jesus is common, which is hard for us to hear. Some are named María Jesús, and María de la Cruz (Mary of the Cross).

Domingo had pleaded with Chris to let him do the wiring to help him maintain his little family. But Domingo wasn't an electrician at all, and not even close to being one. Every switch and plug gave us shocks, and on one occasion I had even been thrown to the floor. When we eventually find someone else to check it, after a million 'mañanas,' they are horrified expressing they are amazed no one has been killed because of the grave mistakes in the wiring, which had no earth whatsoever. But even when wired correctly, the electricity can only be described as weird. Bulbs pop on and off, and stay off most nights. Candles are still necessary.

Then there's the truck to empty our septic tank, which Pepe had said was simple. But there is no indication when the septic tank is full, and we discover there is just one 'pozo-man' (septic tank man) to cover every little village in this vast mountainous region, and he has to be searched out. So we need our chemical toilet again, which had already been joyfully stored away, and which Chris had been tempted to bury for good along with our rubbish the day we moved into the Centro.

Apart from living under a roof instead of in a caravan, we are doing all the same backward things.

Our lives revolve around two men: the pozo-man, the water man. Chris even longs for a third man in our lives – a rubbish man, as he is fed up of having to dig a deep hole every single day in rock hard ground to bury our bag of rubbish, to keep rats and mice at bay.

I must remember something about an escape route in the future. In a battle, the enemy can lay a false escape route – as a trap. I will have to make sure that when I am presented again with an escape route, to be certain that it is the escape route the Lord has sent along, so I don't get discouraged and disappointed.

However, Chris and I are becoming absolute experts in 'his' and 'her' ministries, as everything here is divided into 'she jobs' and 'he jobs.' He the expert 'hole-digger' – she the expert 'clothes-rubber'. Not the true purpose of our call.

"That the testing of your faith produces patience" (endurance; perseverance). James 1:3.

What awful words. Patience. Endurance. Perseverance. And they come *after* the testing of faith!

But I am reminded of the incredible example of that upright and perfect man Job who said, "Shall we indeed accept good from God and not accept adversity (the unexpected)" Job 2:10.

It could take faith… to resign to the unexpected.

7

It Could Take Faith…

to choose

The Civil Guards order us to come out of the house. We think we are in trouble for our Christian sign, but we are told to roll up our sleeves and to get in line with everyone else. There are more than just two civil guards overseeing this task, each with their machine gun. It discourages anyone who would like to question or object – like us. Indifference, following orders, and childlike obedience has been a way of life for these people for decades. They know that objecting won't get them anywhere except in prison. Everyone gives in to whatever without any thought of questioning anything. Their lives are so simple and so lacking in pleasure. Something as ordinary as a haircut draws a crowd as it fills in a few hours of a day. Today's activity seems like a picnic. This is the most cheerful we have seen them yet.

At last, we are all told the reason we are all lined up. Typhoid has broken out! Jabs are compulsory. No questions asked. It is tragic seeing how something medical has made these peasants feel of some importance. They aren't one bit bothered like we are at being punctured by the biggest fattest needle on earth. They are frequent visitors to a doctor, for the most minor problem. It seems they get a feeling of value by it, or are hypochondriacs. Children can almost live at the doctor's surgery, with a sniffle or scratch. They even receive comfort from having an injection, or being handed big suppositories, or huge pills, as it makes them feel protected from some deadly disease. A doctor here is a very busy and tired man.

We haven't heard anything about anyone having typhoid. Chris and I whisper to each other that it could be a trick and that we could be being injected with anything. But how do you question anything when they are the ones with the bullets?

The doctor who is going to give all of these jabs is old and his hands tremble. He is no hurry in between each injection as we stand on burning hot ground without shade as he talks to each Guard underneath the palm tree. The method of injections is nothing less than Victorian. We are the only ones feeling indignant at what is going to happen to us. I am sure the needle is thicker than some of my knitting needles.

The doctor has a helper. He is the person who boils the needle over a little Bunsen burner after each jab while the doctor and guards chat. So we are all going to be pierced with the same needle! We will be here all day as there is a line of at least thirty people. The helper is also the person who knocks the end off each tiny glass bottle of serum and passes it to the doctor. I am trying to hold Calvin's attention in the hope that he hasn't seen the doctor give an injection in one go as yet. The peasants chuckle about it, while we are the only ones with sour faces, making us seem like weak spoiled foreigners.

I fear that such a long needle will go right out the other side of Calvin's skinny arm. I want Calvin to go before me, as my phobia of needles will make me more than flinch at this one. I can't risk Calvin seeing his Mom panic, making a fool of herself, so that he won't want to go. But Calvin's bigger fear than an injection is suppositories. It is the only thing he really moans about here. He dreads the huge torpedo-like things. They are given for fever, pain, and anything and everything, and are handed out to parents like sweets.

I stare at all the glass tops from the serum bottles piling up on the floor, bringing it nearer our turn. I wish we had the courage to object. I'd rather have the typhoid, but there's no choice. Choice is something that has been stolen from these people; what God created them to have.

If only it could be the nice, tender-hearted doctor friend of ours giving these injections, the one who adores children, and is compassionate, instead of one without adequate spectacles, and who has no interest or desire in trying to make an injection quick or painless.

It is Calvin's turn and I am proud as he bravely steps forward. I stare at the back of his shiny blond hair, which stands out amongst the crowd, as I don't want to see him jabbed twice over. I feel overcome by the isolated life he is living. Loneliness for me too, is becoming intolerable. Being here has uncovered an even greater weakness than that of bugs, which is a surprise to me. Wherever we have been, my heart sinks on turning the bend, arriving back at the Centro. I find it an isolated, lonely, and frighteningly dark spot. In England I was used to people, lights, sounds. Daytimes are bearable, but the night-times are long drawn out nightmares for me. We had made contact with quite a few travellers, and because there are no iron bars on our windows, and because we don't know if travellers are to be feared as yet, we aren't certain as to how safe we are each eerie, dark, owl-hooting night.

Calvin's separated life from playmates at the Centro is my new concern. "Every boy needs friends," I keep saying to the Lord." How I regret the selfish decision I made never to have any more children after Calvin was born, even though I adored babies and children. I had loved my days travelling around England as a children's evangelist. I even had a soft spot for unruly children, and received many a comment about the knack the Lord had given me of getting them to change and enjoy a children's meeting.

Yet because my first pregnancy had been difficult, being sick for an entire nine months, and needing injections to halt the sickness because the heaving was straining my tummy, I didn't want another pregnancy. Then the trauma of childbirth doubly confirmed it was something I could live without. Blood tests and hospitals for nine months aren't my cup of tea. Each one of my sisters was a qualified nurse, so I had always felt the odd one out, and as if I was letting the side down. My sisters used to get me to read through the questions for them to prepare for their nursing exams. I would feel faint at pictures of blood, stitches, and bones, and be told I was soft. My Mom suffered the same phobia. I hated this weakness about myself, as I had always wanted more children.

However, when Calvin was three, and we received a call to be missionaries, I felt sorry that he would be an only child, separated from aunts, uncles, grandparents, and cousins. So it gave me the courage to go back on my decision of not to have any more children, so I started having another baby. Sadly, the gap between the boys is a big one, and although Calvin dotes on his baby brother, he is no play-mate yet. Even a T.V. a comic, or a new book would help me feel Calvin was receiving some form of stimulation. The knowledge that he will begin school soon is of no comfort.

--oOo--

I breathe a sigh of relief when the doctor injects Calvin with just one painful jab. We are still not convinced that we have been injected for typhoid. It's hard to trust a country of guns and notepads.

Calvin is proving to be a brilliant little helper in our ministry. We take the children to every outreach or cave, having no one to leave them with anyway. But I would feel it would be a waste of living here if I had to stay at home with the children and not be a part of this calling. It would be unacceptable anyhow, as it is distasteful here to ever see a child as an intrusion. To leave them behind instead of wanting to show them off to everyone would be a huge unforgivable mistake.

A source of great admiration is how many children a couple have. The more they have, the greater they are esteemed. I am almost seen as a flop for only having two, but I am given the benefit of the doubt by some as Wesley isn't 12 months old yet. But it is as if a woman who isn't pregnant isn't normal. I can't seem to pluck up courage to disappoint them to tell them that this is absolutely it!

Children here are never ever put in their place, whatever they do. The more mischievous a child, the more endearing they are. The entire world stops for a child, and it would be unacceptable to acknowledge a parent before the child. Every little girl is a Queen, every little boy a King. Wesley only has to squeak, and I am reprimanded if he isn't immediately snatched up from his pushchair. So I am having to spoil him.

There is nothing to give a child materialistically, so attention is the best they can give. Anyone's child is a source of entertainment. We know that our children will grow up spoiled. It's a worry that I have everything right before going anywhere, but especially to evangelize, wanting to get everything right. I am scolded time and again that the baby's blanket isn't folded right, his sunhat isn't big enough, the hood of the pushchair isn't tilted right, the baby isn't lying in a proper position, or that I have him outdoors at the wrong time of day. To English parents it would be very rude to interfere in this way. But a parent here would feel extremely hurt and left out if no one interfered with the upbringing of their child. They receive great pleasure from it.

The most difficult parts of our services are the disruptions of the many children. Just as we feel we have reached a crucial point and are getting somewhere, or see a spark of interest from someone we least expected it from, there is some disruption from a child, which is amusement to the adults.

But Calvin is always ready to do his part during the services, and watches over his brother and plays games with the children, while I play the accordion. He is very aware of what we are trying to do. Chris and I have decided to relax, and to realize that we are sowing, and the rest isn't our job.

Mountain cave evangelism is our main ministry. Cave ministry is time-consuming. It can take an entire day just to have reached one solitary cave we spotted in the fold of a mountain. There is no route to most so we make our own track through sheer empty wilderness. Regardless of how carefully we have written down clues of how to get back down from a mountain cave, or for a return visit, we get lost over and again and sometimes never find our way back to the same one, but then often discover another cave we wouldn't have known was there. All cave dwellers are not gypsies, but all are destitute, totally isolated, and have a very hard life. They have to grow everything they need to survive, and walk miles for a little water.

Our aim is to hold a Gospel meeting in each cave in the region and to leave a Bible in each. It will be the first time they have ever seen or handled a Bible or heard the Gospel and songs about the Lord. We also take clothes sent to us from England, to relieve a little of their poverty. In the meetings we always include Calvin and Pepe's favourite song, "Yo Tengo Un Amigo Que Me Ama," and because of it, we have been nicknamed by children. Whenever they spot us arriving, they shout "Mire! Es 'el amigo que me ama' que viene." (Look, the friend who loves me is arriving).

The cave people dote on Calvin. Calvin is an ideal missionary child. He has adapted without a whine, any expression of self pity, or moaning – except for suppositories! It was Calvin's desire to give out literature – because he wanted people to find the Lord – which had impressed Pepe so much, Calvin being just a little boy.

We have been invited to return regularly to one particular cave. It is a place teaming with wild dogs, geese, chickens, and cats. The other types of livestock inside the cave convinces me more and more how excellent the Lord is at training and changing people – especially as how I am a cleanaholic, a clutter-free freak, and thrive on order and organization. I have to keep to my daily 'to do' list if it kills me. But this cave is still the worst and the most eerie to get accustomed to. They have old dusty stuffed wild animals perched on high shelves and their glassy eyes gaze down, making us feel spooked. Mice jump to and fro from behind cupboards as we sing, and the lizards by the dozen seem to be part of the family. Food is forced upon us before a meeting, during a meeting, after a meeting. There is absolutely no refusing it.

I cannot understand how our children haven't been ill as yet; everyone force feeds them. Calvin is given the most strangest of treats, like 'fruit' off a cactus. Yet Calvin will have a go at trying anything, and is quickly starting to acquire a taste for whatever he is offered.

On one occasion, we journey further than intended in search of caves, and it gets too late to get back home. We sleep in the car on an old camp ground, intending to head home the next day. The camp ground is neglected and has a filthy toilet, and the whole place is plastered in flies. The next evening Wesley starts to be ill. So much so, we need a doctor before we can travel back home. We find one in the village, and the doctor begins a process of injections. He says we will need to stay for the entire course. He gives Wesley no less than eleven injections throughout one night! I cannot be convinced that he knows what he is doing so want to leave, and get back to our own doctor.

All the way back home, Wesley is quite ill. Don Pedro isn't at all impressed that we have stayed on a fly-ridden campground. Wesley is getting worse, and now has sickness and diarrhoea and unable to keep down food or drink. Early each morning, a saddened Don Pedro, still too humble and old fashioned to have eye contact with me, comes to our mission-house to inject Wesley.

The preparation for the injection is the same old Victorian style. The thick needle is boiled on an open flame. But what the doctor does next is beyond belief, and as a mother I am rigid with disapproval. He aims the needle at the baby's thigh, and 'throws' it into his leg as if he's a dartboard. Then while the needle sticks out of Wesley's leg, the doctor breaks the end off the glass bottle of serum, and begins to attach the bottle of serum to the needle in the thigh by 'screwing' it on, around and around. Eventually, he pushes the serum down into the needle. Trying to keep a baby still, while all this palaver is happening, is torture. The procedure is an unbelievable insight into the dark ages, yet it is so sad to hear so many times, how they live in the best country in the world and that it has the best food on earth. Some even say to us, that we have really only come for their sun and food. We feel it is either comforting for them to block out, or they are truly brainwashed.

Every morning, the doctor arrives to go through the exact same gruesome routine. I dread the door knocking each morning. Wesley isn't getting any better, and seems to be getting worse. He lies sad and still in his cot, with gastroenteritis type symptoms – although we haven't been told what is actually wrong with him.

I read Hebrews again, and notice that faith was different things to people. For Noah and Abraham, faith had been obeying. For Sarah, faith had been believing. But for Moses and Rahab – faith had been *choosing*. It is the *choosing* that grabs my attention.

The next day, the doctor arrives, and as usual starts preparing to boil the needle. I have to pluck up the courage, to tell this gentle man I don't want the baby to have any more injections. He is visibly upset, and asks me if I am aware of what I am saying and for the first time, looks me straight in the eye, his eyes filling with tears. I assure him that I do.

It isn't that I think it wrong to use doctors. I believe in Christians receiving treatment to get well, for as long as a hospital or doctor can offer it, but I can see Wesley isn't benefiting, and that a choice has to be made.

The doctor leaves, making clear that the injections are still needed. As I inspect the blue, purple, and green bruises all over Wesley's tiny white legs, I tell Chris I have no doubt that the right choice has been made.

The next day there is an incredible change, and Wesley is his lively, giggling self, and above all, he is dry.

My view of faith is changing. The Bible examples I see of faith were far from arrogant demands or expectations. I don't believe that faith is an emotional weapon to try and manipulate what I want from the Almighty. I don't see faith any more that treats God as a waiter, where I give the orders, and expect Him to carry them out. That would be God being my servant, and as ridiculous as clay telling a potter what to do.

Jesus taught that faith, had to be honest. He asked a blind man what he could see after He had had laid hands on him. If the blind man hadn't answered truthfully – that he saw men as trees walking – he would have seen men walking as trees forever! But he was honest enough to say he wasn't healed when Jesus asked him. So Jesus touched him again, and he was healed (Mark 8:24).

Also, the faith in the Bible never assumed. Faith was a gentle appeal. The leper said: "*If* you are *willing...*' (Matthew 8:2).

Shadrach, Meshach, and Abed-nego said, "Our God will deliver us, but *if* He *does not...*" So faith isn't presumption, a word which the dictionary describes as: insolence; arrogance; disrespectful; over confident.

If God made me in His image, and I have choice, why would I invent a God who is a robot? And if I wouldn't like others to make decisions for me, why would I expect to make them for God? If I wouldn't like being taken for granted, what would make me think God would?

When David was in trouble, he said, "*Let* Your hand be ready to help me, for I have chosen Your precepts" (Psalm 119:173).

David had chosen these 'precepts' a long time before he made his desperate and humble appeal to God for help. But he still didn't see any right to command, presume, or order.

The 'precepts' David had chosen were: God's ways; God's instructions; God's laws; God's principles; God's ways; God's mandates; God's rules.

It could take faith… to choose them.

8

—

It Could Take Faith...

to keep quiet

It can't be true!

Who will I have to talk to? If only there were other missionaries around to chat to about this. It has made me feel more stranded, and lonelier than ever.

This means I will have to stay at home while Chris evangelizes the caves. We have got quite used to making our own tracks to the caves and have had many a laugh whenever we have got lost, and had learned to always have emergency food in the car. Now, I will have to miss it all.

But, there is no doubt, the sickness has already started. I am pregnant. I can't stand the thought of being pregnant in the middle of nowhere, and just as I was beginning to adapt to cave ministry. I am ashamed to say, I wouldn't mind some of that 'official help' now. Being pregnant without a clinic, modern facilities, and being so far from a city is daunting.

But knowing without doubt I am pregnant, I make the decision, to start asking God for something. I start praying,

"Lord, please let it be a little girl." This lonely detached wilderness could be brightened up with a little daughter all dolled up in pretty pink frilly dresses.

I had always wanted a brother, so I had been anything but disappointed when I achieved a second son, always having imagined how sons are the ones who protect their Moms when they are old.

Now, regardless of the female task here of carrying water on heads, I crave a daughter. I fill my days praying morning 'til night, day in day out, pleading, begging, and appealing to the Lord just how much it would mean. I'm sure heaven must be tired of hearing the same words, like when Chris kept coming back from the post office repeating, "Just the holes."

It is my first experience of constantly beseeching and pleading to the Lord without any thought of giving up, or even wondering if it is His will. All I know is, that I want a girl badly enough, I can't even reason that way.

I recall how many times I had given up on a prayer when it hadn't been answered immediately. How did I expect God to take a prayer seriously if it hadn't been important enough for me not to go on to another?

My hope to receive a baby girl is driven by a story in the Bible. A widow bothered a judge for so long, the judge eventually gave in to what she wanted just to get some peace (Luke 18). I'd also been impressed by the single mindedness of sick people in the Bible. A blind man wasn't going to be put off because Jesus hadn't responded to his first cry. The blind man could have sighed in acceptance, but he didn't and received his sight.

Faith for me this time will be, to keep on appealing. I am being encouraged by a scripture, "Ask and it shall be given you," because I have noticed in the Bible index that its true meaning is – to keep *on* asking.

As I get bigger, I ache to know what position the baby is lying, something every mother-to-be longs to know. So Chris takes me to see Don Pedro to find out. I am still called the 'preacher protestante's' wife, which has severed me from certain female privileges in this dark culture, and I have a feeling that a personal examination will be another.

On answering the door, the doctor goes through all his usual military style procedure, and I hope I am wrong about my assumption. As usual his attention goes straight to the boys, who love visiting the doctor's house because of all the fuss they receive. Here, it is the adults who play second fiddle to their children. It is an insight as to how children must feel in England, when they have to be the invisible ones when in the company of adults.

To me, my pregnancy seems normal, even the unending sickness is what I knew it would be. The kicking seems high up, so hopefully it is because the baby is already in the birth position. But I long to be sure.

How I yearn for a chat to another English pregnant mom, to compare sizes of tummies, and to talk of all things pregnant. At least getting ready to go somewhere, to talk to someone about my pregnancy, has given me a feeling that my pregnancy is receiving some interest.

Chris explains to Don Pedro how I would like to know what position the baby is in. Poor Don Pedro! He looks as if he is going to die of embarrassment. But he calls in Concepción. I am thrilled. I am going to be examined, because Don Pedro always calls in his wife if ever it is me who needs any medical attention. I am going to know what I have longed to know. But we can't believe what happens next. Don Pedro settles himself back comfortably in his worn, green leatherette chair. Then he says to Chris,

"Mire Cristóbal, es muy fácil" (Look Christopher, it's very simple). Then Don Pedro rolls his own hand over his own tubby tummy saying, "Es así" (it's like this). I watch disappointed as he explains to Chris, how the hardest part of the 'bump' should be at the lowest part of the tummy. Then he asks Chris, "Entiende Cristóbal?" (Do you understand Christopher?) I can't believe it when I hear Chris answer yes! All of this portrays another of the cultural things we have had to get used to. Men avoid speaking to, or addressing a woman. If a woman were to ask any man a question, which would be rude anyway, the answer would be given to her husband.

As the doctor continues with his self examination, it's hard for Chris and me not to laugh. But I try to absorb my medical lesson, via Chris, in self-examination. We leave knowing that I am not going to get the attention I need in this pregnancy. When I try to copy the examination lesson at home, the 'bump' still seems the same all over to me. I just have to hope that the movements high up my rib-cage, causing the awful heartburn, are legs, not arms.

One day, after months and months of my usual prayer, "Please, please, be merciful Lord, and give me a girl," I can't continue asking. Suddenly, it feels like a waste of time. It seems as if I am repeating it for no reason. The prayer feels different, like a dead meaningless request, and I don't get why a sudden blank wall. But every waking moment as I begin my prayer, there is an inexplicable emptiness, and a heaviness that I shouldn't be asking any more. Then one day, I get it. I understand. I'm having a girl! The family believe me when I say she is on the way, and we speak about her as part of the family. I am especially thrilled that it is a girl, as Chris already had the third name ready if a boy, even though he had chosen our sons' names. He was going to call the third Luther!

When Chris chose Calvin's name, Chris noticed how Churches back in England had stopped asking him to preach. So then he chose Wesley for our second son, and Chris was pleased the Churches asked him to preach again. I had wanted Calvin to be called Lloyd, but I had to be satisfied with it being Calvin Lloyd. Then I had wanted our second son to be called Adam, but I had to be satisfied with it being Wesley Adam. So I am particularly thrilled that we are having a girl. But in true Chris style, as soon as he knows a daughter is on the way, he is planning the name again! I am beginning to think I may have a bossy hubby.

I had wanted to call our daughter Carmen, but some missionaries had somehow heard about it and written to us. The letter said that we must not call our baby Carmen at any cost. I was disappointed, but the advice was stern. The missionaries explained that it was the name of a worshipped Saint here, so it wouldn't look good for a missionary to name their child after an idol. We didn't want to offend the missionaries as they had taken the trouble to advise inexperienced missionaries like us, so we had to forget Carmen, much to my disappointment.

In my pregnant state I am still able to visit a few caves, even if only to thrill the women. I must show them that I am as normal as they, with my big tum. But I can't be of much help playing my accordion over my bump, so they are missing the music. My pregnancy is going down a treat though. It has made a lot of difference in being more accepted, and especially by some who were sceptical of us.

However, I am beginning to get some unusual physical discomfort. I have developed a strong stitch in my side, making it more painful than usual when I am sick. I eventually have to take to sitting in a chair, not going anywhere, and cough my way through most days.

Chris decides that he can't leave me alone at an isolated Centro without our vehicle when he goes out on cave ministry, so he buys an old motorbike from someone. This isn't a happy time for Chris. It takes him over an hour to get to one particular cave who rely on his visits, then the same back, and the bike isn't a reliable one. The journeys are long, hard, bumpy rides through dark wilderness and riverbeds. He is in agony with his buttocks. I am always so relieved to hear him arriving back home. He always has funny tales to tell us. At one particular cave, a woman told him to be careful when he is riding through a certain field to get to their cave. She said he should look out for the bald trail where no weeds or scrub grow. She explained that the reason for the bald trail was because it was where a man had killed someone and then had dragged the body through the fields, and the path had remained barren ever since. Every time after that, when Chris is returning from that cave, and has to go over the bald trail, he says he never thought an old bike could go so fast!

I am getting weaker. Then it feels something is really wrong when my breathing gets difficult. So Chris has to ask Doctor Pedro to come and see me. He is concerned and his diagnosis is startling. He says I have Bronco-Pneumonia! He said that if I were not pregnant, the condition could quite easily be cured, as stronger drugs could be used. Anyway, he says he will still start me on daily injections to relieve the condition.

I am horrified that it is me going to be the dartboard, but all my objections to the doctor, and my fear and panic is ignored, and the doctor is even amused by it.

The doctor begins the dreaded procedure, Chris, and Concepción always having to be present.

But I am not getting any better, and the doctor says

it is because I need much stronger treatment, yet seems reluctant to give it. Then one day, out of the blue, the doctor tells Chris to get me to England as soon as possible! We tell him it is impossible. I am not only seven months pregnant, but we know nothing about flying out of here as yet. We try to reason with him, to no avail. I had only ever been on one little short plane ride, from England to Ireland, and to suddenly be told to get a flight alone, from somewhere we hardly know anything about, at such a late stage of a pregnancy, is frightening. But the doctor insists and offers help with arrangements.

We arrive at the airport, after a painful, smouldering hot three hour journey, on twisting narrow roads, me being sick and coughing all the way. As I board the plane with little Wesley, I hold up a book to hide my face so the staff don't see how poorly I am. My eyes fill with tears as I look back at Calvin and his Dad from the steps, knowing how they will feel when they arrive back to a dead, lifeless wilderness, without Wesley and me. The only way I receive strength to live like this is by believing God wants us to. And I do know that the lessons I have learned so far, do outweigh anything I go through. I am still grateful for the privilege, and amazed at God's humility to train, and not discard, giving grace to such an 'un-missionary' type, when I know how there are ready-made 'proper missionaries' – as I always call them.

My Mom and Dad are at Birmingham airport to collect Wesley and me. I am shocked at the sharp gush of wet, cold, icy wind, but I feel clean and fresh for the first time in years, and can immediately breathe better. Mom's first words as she throws thick blankets around us are moans about the terrible weather, and I suddenly remember what it is that every English person grumbles about – the

English weather. But I love every goose bump, which almost irritates Mom.

When I arrive at the hospital, the nurses are annoyed at my lack of prenatal care, even objecting to me having a bed because they haven't been the ones monitoring me. I haven't the courage to tell them, that I haven't been monitored by anyone at all as yet. It doesn't take long for me to catch on how my glowing sun tan, amongst every pale face, stands out, and how it portrays a carefree life of sunshine in a romantic Spain, and how lucky I am only to have returned for medical attention. There is an attitude that I am completely unprepared for. It feels like having run to a place of solace, hurting, and in distress, just to be rejected. The stinging remark, "Why do missionaries always seem to choose the *hot* places?" makes me feel like a stranger in my own country, and I realize that I don't belong anywhere any more.

I had quite forgotten how much the wet, and dismal climate of my home-land terribly affects my race. How I would love to tell them that the sun isn't everything, and that Spain isn't the dream place that holiday brochures portray. How I would like for them to know not to make the same mistake as me of not enjoying England, and that it is better to be drenched in rain every day, than scorch to death with lizards, scorpions, centipedes, snakes, and huge spiders. It's a pity to see them with a 'grass is greener' syndrome. I would like for them to know what it has taken for me to realize what a lovely, free, clean country England is, where no one is spied upon every day, and that but for feeling called – Spain would be the last place on earth to live. I want to tell them to appreciate something as ridiculous as a dustbin man, drinking water at the touch of a tap, soft towels, and to be happy about living in a country of washing machines.

But I never ever thought that faith… could be keeping quiet.

Because I know if I do say all of this, it will just come over as a missionary who is after some sympathy and attention, as I have already come over as smug, conceited, and self-satisfied, and like a 'goody two shoes'. It is because I am seemingly appreciating such silly things. While everyone else in their hospital bed complains about hospital meals, I am in absolute heaven, enjoying every mouthful, but trying not to show it, as it makes them seem ungrateful. But the smell of the food, long before it arrives, drives me wild. Then there's the trolley! Digestive biscuits. Chocolate bars. Crisps. English newspapers. Shampoo that actually lathers. The toilets flush properly, and there are – toilet rolls. There's also a brand new incredible invention since we had left – TELEVISION IN COLOUR!

My beaming face while I lie in my hospital bed is embarrassing me. I never thought hospital could be so entertaining. Even the doctor doesn't seem too happy that I am not too upset about being ill, and especially when my husband isn't around. I relax in crisp white cotton sheets, writing list after list of things to take back to the wilderness – moisture creams, sunglasses, fly-spray, bug-powder, disinfectant, tea-bags, gravy mix, toilet rolls, sweets, and books and toys. It's hard trying to fight off being happy that Don Pedro insisted I come back to England.

The rain is discussed all day by patients and staff, while I sympathize. But I love watching it splashing against the windows and landing on fresh green grass. The clean neat streets lined with lights, and the cosy houses look heavenly.

Each time the dinner trolley arrives, I try to appear unmoved, but I am tucking into my meal before the others have even lifted the dome to peep what's underneath it.

They plonk the dome down in disgust, and sigh at me as if I have let the side down.

That postal strike had taught me to give thanks for most things, but it's easy to give thanks for cottage pie smothered in gravy instead of an alcachofa leaf.

Although I am thoroughly enjoying my illness, I have had a lot of time to think. I am beginning to regret something. I regret that we had ever shared Chris's dream. Even though we had found a real place called Cuevas and caves, it is becoming increasingly embarrassing explaining why we aren't actually living there. Whatever reasons I give sound like excuses.

That dream became too important, and we are to blame. I am wondering if we are guilty of having exposed private, spiritual details, to people it wasn't meant for. It was a dream of guidance from a merciful heavenly Father, because we were going somewhere that without it, we would never have known existed. I feel it is wrong now, to make personal guidance known to others. It could have stumbled them, wounded us, and even disappointed God.

I start to think, how God deals with each of his children in a different way, and how that each person is distinct, and how a personal relationship with Him – should be personal. If God did the same with everyone, there would be no individuality. No other person had needed our dream. It had been a message for us. I can also see how telling personal things from God, could cause pride, and feelings of spiritual superiority. It could also make others feel of less importance, or left out.

It could take faith… to keep quiet.

More than anything, I would like God to be able to trust me. If husbands and wives have secrets that aren't to be shared with anyone else – why not God, if we are made in his image? I didn't want to be the person to whom God could never reveal anything because I couldn't keep it quiet, or because I needed to prove God had spoken to *me*. Mary the Mother of Jesus was a great example. She had the biggest revelation ever, but had the maturity to "ponder it in her heart."

I had come to a new conclusion in my walk with the Lord; a private word or revelation should be private. It doesn't have to be shared with everyone, like I had always believed.

"In QUIETNESS and trust is your strength." (Isaiah 3:15). I had never thought that a closed mouth could make someone strong.

I can't believe what I am seeing! Chris and Calvin have arrived! They have driven right through Spain and France hoping to make it for the birth. They have! I'm in labour.

"It's a girl," the midwife says, waiting to hear a sigh of relief from me knowing I have two sons.

I had known however for a long time what my first question would be when she was born, "Is she coughing?" I really thought that because I had coughed my way through most of my pregnancy that she would automatically be born with a cough.

The midwife thought I'd gone completely mad, and snapped, "Cough? Coughing? What on earth do you mean Mrs Smith? Of course she isn't coughing. Don't be so silly. She's a gorgeous, 8 lb 8oz, healthy baby girl. Now what are you going to call her?"

"Her name is Cherry Raquel," Chris promptly pipes up – just in case 'Eve' popped out first, because I wanted an 'Eve' when I couldn't have a Carmen. Chris had been present for the birth, but how I wish he hadn't been. In his own way he had tried to make me laugh throughout labour, by putting his hospital mask across one eye. Then he had stood on one leg saying, "Ha. Ha. Jim Hawkins" (the one-legged pirate). The midwife had been livid.

It is June twenty fourth 1973. Cherry Raquel has arrived – both of her names having been chosen by my bossy husband.

The Lord has so graciously given me my hearts desire, and what I had pleaded and begged for, a daughter, and a sister for Calvin and Wesley. I am more than ready to keep my part and take her back to brighten up our wilderness, to walk alone, die to self, to be brave, to be a help-meet, to give thanks, adjust to the unexpected, to choose…

…or just to keep plain quiet.

We arrive back in Spain with our one month old beautiful bundle all dolled up in pink, and take her immediately to see Doctor Pedro and Concepción. There is absolute delight, even though they are confused why Cherry hadn't had her ears pierced at birth, and say how she will get mistaken for a boy. They have gifts ready waiting. We open two exquisitely wrapped boxes. Inside the first, a delicate gold cross on a gold chain, and inside the second, a tiny gold baby bangle. What a welcome.

Welcome to the mission-field Cherry Raquel.

9

It Could Take Faith...

to wait

The day for Calvin to start school can't be delayed for much longer. While we had been in England for the baby's birth he had mixed with boys his own age and had loved it. Apart from the language, he still has huge obstacles to face for the very first foreign boy to start school here. I dread it. We set a date, still determined to keep our brood together.

I decide to spend time outside the school, to observe the routine. I need to take note of what the children wear, what they eat, what they do. I have to make sure that Calvin will fit in as much as possible. I notice how the only thing to distinguish a little boy from a little girl, is that every girl wears earrings, as they all dress identical, in trousers and green and white striped smocks. Girls have their ears pierced a few days after birth. But I don't think I will ever be able to have Cherry's ears pierced as I couldn't take seeing a needle go through her ear lobe. Also, earrings are considered sinful back home. So she will have to be the odd one out when she begins school.

It has been impossible to find a teacher or parent willing to advise me beforehand, on where to get all the things Calvin needs to start school. It is clear they aren't going to be of any encouragement.

At playtime I watch as each child feverishly unwraps an identical 'bocadillo' which is a whole bar of bread stuffed with fiery red 'chorizo', like Pepe adored. The playground smells of it.

Calvin is getting excited. Chris and I have decided not to warn him of anything the missionaries had told us about. We don't want to make him nervous, but we wouldn't know exactly what to warn him of anyway, not having a clue what will happen. It brings little comfort that at last Calvin will have company. I can't help but feel sorry for him. It is my first-born's first day at school, a day I had always looked forward to. I never dreamed it would be in a foreign school in dictatorship regime.

Calvin sits grinning in the car clutching his little brown satchel with a strong smell of chorizo coming from it. He peers through the window looking for the sight of children, totally unaware of any problems awaiting him. It will be six hours before we know how things have been for him. The missionaries words come to mind, "Unkind and cruel," making me feel a terrible Mom.

Is it me being selfish to want to keep the children with us instead of sending them to England? Is faith letting them go? Or is faith keeping them? Please let faith be keeping them.

Calvin runs to the gate happy to see so many children, all looking like him, except for being the only blond head. I am pleased I had got everything right.

I am so relieved now Calvin is out of the car to be able to bawl my eyes out, and can't help but cry all the way home. I had always looked forward to Calvin's first day at school, like it portrays in children's books; rosy-faced teachers welcoming first-timers to school, comforting any parent who is upset. Instead, he won't understand a thing.

For the first few days, Calvin seems baffled as to what is happening. He talks about strange repetitive rituals which go on throughout most of the day, and because he is the only child not doing them, it is causing disruption. He tells us he doesn't want to do anything contrary to scripture, so is glad that he doesn't know how to do them. He says how complicated they are, yet seem like ABC to the other children.

Eventually, the message is clear that they are trying to get Calvin out of the school. It will be for security of their jobs, and for continuing respect and acceptance in a tiny village, to make life uncomfortable for the first foreigner and preacher's son. It is so sad to see such a kindly natured little boy, being discriminated against. I am crushed knowing how he has already endured separation, boredom, and hardship in his new isolated surroundings. How I wish they all knew, even cared, about what it has been like for him and just how brave and co-operative he has been.

Then Calvin is made to sit apart from everyone else in the class. The other children know it isn't in their favour to try to be friends with him. Then one day, we find out that it has been announced to the whole class, "Calvin is a rebellious and discourteous boy, of some foreign, wicked religion."

In my role as a missionary, this is my toughest experience yet. Our child is being publicly shown to be a bad influence. Calvin sits, and sits, each day, ignored, lonely, bored, and hurt. It feels like some plan to try and get rid of us all, because I know how much this race love children. They know only too well, how moms cannot take watching their child, or any child, suffer. We are shocked how Calvin has been so loved by cave people, yet so unaccepted and despised at school. We see the school as just a place for conditioning children to a system.

I start to doubt about coming to a mission-field independently. I crave now to be in some kind of organization. We need expert advice and help. Yet I know their convictions could be quite different from ours, and could suggest sending Calvin away like others had been. Yet I know we can't sort it by ourselves. It's as if there is no answer to it. It is devastating knowing a charming little boy isn't being treated properly. My heart aches all day, every day.

I begin to think what if things never change! What if it is that 'thorn in the flesh' – that 'unanswered prayer' that Paul the Apostle had to live with? We had heard so many preachers and Christians talk about their particular 'thorn in the flesh', that it almost seemed unspiritual not to have one.

Then Calvin did something unwise without realising. He thought it would help, but it made things worse for him. Without our knowledge, he took it on himself, to put a bundle of Spanish Gospel tracts in his satchel, and gave them out at school. He said he had done it because he wanted people to know Jesus. The teacher flipped, and spat on the leaflets for all the children to see.

It is obvious that this tiny village school will not risk change, and will fight any foreign influence, and they have the entire Police State behind them to back them up.

I start to define our call. We know without doubt that we would not be here if we didn't feel passionately that

God had called us to be. So reason says why try and get out of a situation a call of God causes? If God's will causes inconvenience and adversity, then faith must be going through them.

As young as Calvin is he knows the reason we are here, and he helps in every way. He has believed in us. He has trusted us. He is persevering even though craving to be accepted and be part of them.

I just long to tell those teachers what Jesus said, "Whoever offends a child would be better a millstone…" and "Suffer the little children to come unto me…" I long to tell them we will be going home, and that they will remain in their backward ways forever.

However – dying to self means dying to what I feel like doing. I can think of only one thing *to* do, as there is nothing else. But it is something I am hopeless at. Maybe, faith could be *waiting*.

It could take faith… to wait.

We will hang on. We will wait. We will pray,
"Is anyone among you suffering? Then he must pray." (James 5:13)

I never knew, until now, that doing nothing, or standing still, and feeling useless, or – waiting – could be called 'works'. It is the hardest 'work' I have ever had to do. I am not a 'waiter'. If anything needs doing, I have to get it done. If there is a problem, I have to sort it out. I am anything but laid back. I am so motivated, Chris can hardly keep up, and slow Spain has made me feel as if I am living life backwards.

Every day, we drive to school, and every day, we pick up Calvin, I have to stop myself from jumping from the car to speak with the teachers. But I have to remind myself that the 'works' of waiting – doesn't do a thing.

I remind myself of seven things while waiting for the Lord.

1. <u>To wait in silence.</u> "My soul waits in silence" (Psalm 62:1). "It is good that he waits silently" (Lamentations 3:25, 26).

2. <u>To plead with the Lord</u>, being humble about it. "O Lord, be gracious to us; we have waited for You" (Isaiah 33:2).

3. <u>Not to get impatient</u>, "They did not wait... so He gave them their request, but sent..."(Psalm 106:13)

4. <u>To wait in hope</u>, and rest. "Those who hopefully wait for Me will not be put to shame"(Isaiah 49:23). "Rest (lit: be still) in the Lord and wait patiently (lit: longingly) for Him" (Psalm 37:7).

5. <u>To remind oneself</u>. "And now, Lord, for what do I wait?" (Psalm 39:7).

6. <u>To look eagerly</u>. "I will look eagerly for Him." (Isaiah 8:17).

7. <u>To expect action</u>. "Who acts on behalf of the one who waits for Him" (Isaiah 64:4). I must keep in mind, that this promise is a conditional one. The action is only for those who *wait*.

Suddenly, I feel compassion for the teachers. I have the feeling that they must dislike the way they are behaving. We haven't met one person yet, who is unaffected on seeing a child unhappy. It is just in their nature, and Calvin is so easy to like. They have to be doing something that is more than likely making them as miserable as we are.

The weekends are heavenly, knowing I don't have to fight the flesh for at least two days. But from Monday to Friday, the 'works' of waiting is my biggest battle yet, knowing our son has to endure another week of persecution.

There is just one benefit. Calvin is coming home

teaching us new words in Spanish. But we learn something terrible! That day in Cuevas, when a man told us to find 'EL BORRACHO,' the man was being insulting about the man he had told us to find. 'El Borracho' was not the man's name at all. El Borracho means 'The Drunk!' So we had actually been told to look for 'the drunk,' and we had been enquiring where 'the Drunk' lived! We had even called him 'Mr Drunk'('Señor Borracho') the whole time we had been speaking with him! Now it's clear why he had kept repeating, "I am not a drunk – but I am the person you need to see."

One day, when we collect Calvin from school, something exciting has happened. A boy called Santiago had sat next to him. Calvin's loving magnetic personality had been too intriguing to Santiago. We have also picked up that it is becoming harder for the teachers to keep disciplining the children about all this, and that it is all wearing a little thin.

As time goes on, hearts begin to soften towards our son. He is slowly, but surely, being accepted. Eventually, he even becomes a favourite with the children – even the teachers, and Santiago had started it all off.

I suddenly feel like a normal Mom with a son at school, and can't wait for him to arrive home every day, now not through dread, but excitement, to talk about the normal everyday happenings of a boy's school day. It is the highlight of my day.

During the summer holiday, amazing things happen. I know back home how ridiculous it would be to call something so simple 'amazing', but here it is amazing, because everyone who breathes is monitored, and don't live free lives. The parents of Calvin's now best friend Santiago, take Calvin home to their house to play with him. As usual, whenever Calvin is playing, or wherever he is, he is in the habit of singing his and Pepe's favourite song, "Yo Tengo Un Amigo Que Me Ama, Su Nombre Es Jesús" (I have a friend who loves me, His Name is Jesus).

One day Santiago's Mom and Dad ask if they can drop Santiago off at our house to play with Calvin. As soon as Santiago enters our house he dashes around everywhere as if searching for something in every room under beds and inside cupboards. Santiago is from a very traditional family, like Don Pedro and Concepción, who have the most impeccable traditional manners, and are the essence in politeness. So we are baffled by what Santiago is doing, knowing his Mom would be upset if she knew. Eventually Santiago settles down, yet doesn't look too happy as he and Calvin play, yet is reluctant to tell us the reason. A few weeks later, Santiago's Mom tells us how much he had enjoyed his time with Calvin at our house, once he had got over Calvin's lies, and she laughs. We ask what lies Calvin had told. She chuckles and explains. When Calvin had visited their house he had sung a song over and over, about a friend he had called Jesus, "Yo tengo un amigo que me ama, su nombre es Jesús." So Santiago had boasted to all his friends how he was not only going to the new English boy's house to play, but was also going to make friends with another friend the new foreign boy had, called Jesus. So Santiago had told his Mom how Calvin had been fibbing, because he didn't have another friend at his house at all! Santiago hadn't thought for one moment that Calvin had been singing about the Divine. To Santiago, the name was just another person's name.

Calvin has become popular at school. The Lord has used a little life and a painful experience to change people who weren't comfortable speaking to us before. Until now, we had only witnessed to, and been accepted by gypsies and cave people. Now we are ready to reach another type, and we feel a little sad, that we had only had gypsies and cave dwellers in mind.

Calvin had been the very first foreigner to attend a school at least fifty years behind the times. He had been the first to crack solid ice.

"Indeed, none of those who wait for You will be ashamed" (Psalm 25:3).

I look up the dictionary definition for *wait*, and *ashamed*. Wait is defined as – 'hold on,' and ashamed is defined as – 'sorry.'

I read the scripture again,

"Indeed, none of those who 'HOLD ON' for Thee will be 'SORRY.'

It could take faith… to wait.

10

It Could Take Faith…
to work unnoticed

It can't be true! My Mom is coming over! I've longed for her and Dad to come, but I know Mom will hate it. The cave people are so hospitable, and the hospitality goes with the call, but I know Mom will find it very difficult. Mom's letter says that Dad feels well enough to travel, and that they are making arrangements to come with Chris's Mom, just the three of them, to see their 'baby' missionaries of the family.

At least their visit will mean that Chris and I will be able to go out alone together for the first time on this mission-field – but we'll have to do some head scratching to think where to go. At least the Spanish child idolisers won't disapprove when they see us out as a couple, once they know esteemed grandparents are babysitting.

It is exciting news about our parents' visit. Chris and I had started to wonder if we were getting overlooked in this unknown corner, thinking 'out of sight out of mind.' The children can hardly wait, and their grandparents' visit is dominating our whole conversation as we start out for some cave-work one morning. Chris suddenly swerves on the road, which is nothing new to us, but this time it is to avoid an animal lying dead on a bend. There are all kinds of suggestions of what the unusual animal could be, "It's a tiger. No, no, it's just a big squirrel." Much to our disappointment, Chris won't stop for us to check what it is. He says if the animal isn't quite dead, it could be serious if it bit any one of us. My point is that if it isn't quite dead it could be suffering. So now, instead of our parents dominating our conversation, it is the animal, with Chris keep trying to divert the conversation back to our parents in an attempt to defend himself because we have made him feel mean for not stopping for us to have a look. Eventually, Chris succeeds, and the animal gets forgotten as we go on our way.

We arrive home late after a tiring day of mountain ministry, and as I prepare the children for bed, I start to pity them somewhat. It can't be easy for children to be fully involved in a travelling ministry, being pushed here, there, and everywhere, with strangers ruffling their hair, stroking their face, force feeding them weird food, or being squeezed and kissed forcefully on both cheeks. I also feel for them growing up so fast without aunts, uncles, or grandparents around to see their stages of growth. Losing touch with relatives and cousins bothers me. There is no family interest in them, like other children enjoy, such as pocket money, birthday or Christmas presents. I try not to let these dismal thoughts take hold, and must keep reminding myself how the children will be learning valuable lessons, and how we are growing into a close-knit family. We will probably always have a unique bond, and a reliance on each other.

I wish I didn't feel so much concern that there isn't a real church for our brood, or a Sunday-school, or any other Christian influence. I don't want to be busy 'winning the world', and lose my own sheep, the fruit of my womb. An overwhelming feeling of responsibility comes over me to get our priorities right.

As I tidy up a book is lying open on the floor. It is at a page showing the coloured photograph of an unusual animal which makes me jump. The family appear around me, on seeing it isn't just another lizard that has caused me to gasp. The picture in the book looks identical to the animal Chris swerved to avoid in the morning. Chris picks up the book and reads the title out aloud – "The Civet Cat – a rare wild animal. It's a rare, wild animal Christine!" Then tucking the book underneath his arm he makes his way to the car with, "Come on everybody. Jump in. Let's go and see it."

I object as it is late and it seems silly to expect an animal to still be there after thirteen hours. But no one listens and everyone is already in the vehicle. "Chris," I say, "No one will have swerved to miss a dead animal, like our family of animal lovers. We can't seriously be going just to see flattened flesh – even if it is rare flesh."

But the whole incident has caused too much intrigue. So on the way I read out aloud all about it.

"The Civet Cat"

The civet cat is one of the rarest wild animals today, but used to be quite common in the castles and villages of Europe. It was the mouse catcher.

In the medieval days the household cat was unknown. It was brought to Europe from Africa by the crusaders. The household cat took the civet cat's place and became our fireside pet. The civet cat then went to live in the wild. Not too many people have ever seen a civet cat with its pointed nose, and striped tail. The civet cat is nocturnal, and a creature of the dark. It is a RARE – WILD – ANIMAL."

As we slow down towards the bend, something becomes visible in the headlights. It is the animal. We get out of the car, and it is eerie peering down at a plump body, still all in one piece, and even in the exact same position, as it had been 13 hours earlier.

"It's beautiful Chris," I say, "and it IS a civet cat. Yippee, we have a rare, wild animal."

Chris replies with, "What now then?" He is nearly sick when I ask him to put it in the car, but picks up the limp body by its long bushy striped tail and holds it up high for us all to get a look. Then he flops it onto the floor in the car, and we drive on with dead cold fur between our feet.

I begin to wonder what it's about. A book lying open at the exact page of an animal we had seen lying untouched for 13 hours.

"What are you going to do with it Christine? How long can you keep a dead animal for?" Chris wants answers, even though it was him who wanted to come and see it. Looking at the cat's tiny, jagged teeth, I don't feel it can just be discarded, yet I have no answers. I suggest we take it home until we can think of something.

On the way home we discuss all kinds of things we could do with it. We drive by a lane, which is the lane we use to get to my most hated cave, the one with ancient dusty dead animals and unfriendly geese, and I get an idea. I shout for Chris to turn quickly into the lane. "Let's go there right now Chris. Let's take the animal to Gracia's cave as they may have some idea of what we can do with it." Chris swerves into the lane, and grumbles as if it is the first time he has ever swerved. We start the climb to the highest and most isolated of caves where we have meetings. It is nestled into a mountain top, and is so high up, its whitened entrance can be seen in daytime from all surrounding areas.

"I can't believe we're doing this," Chris says. "It's bad enough driving up to it in daylight. It has to be foolish to go up so late with the children."

I know he is right. Night-time driving can be nerve racking. In such a vast and empty space everywhere looks the same even in daylight. But the whole incident has filled us with curiosity. "It would have to be your favourite cave Christine," Chris says, still trying to put me off. "You know the one you always need the most grace to visit." He is right. I loathe it, even if I have received more grace to cope – and I still need more yet. Apart from all the bug-ridden vicious dogs, we discovered quite by accident, something worse when we arrived too soon for a meeting. The mother was doing weird things to someone in the back of the cave. It was witchcraft! It terrified us, and it was then we realized why she had told Chris the story about the bald trail where no weeds grow. But we are at least welcome there, so it is an opportunity to teach them from scripture that what the mother is doing is wrong. We are not convinced as yet, that Gracia, the thirty-year-old daughter, isn't involved in it also. Gracia is a polio victim. She was two years old when it happened. She is completely withered from the waist down. Her mother told us that she was to blame as she had given her some bad water by mistake. It is heart-rending to see an upper body being pulled along by elbows, while two tiny withered legs drag behind over a filthy dirt floor. We continue to go to the cave for Gracia's sake, as she has expressed a desire to know more about the Bible, but she has also taken to us. Chris treats her like a Queen and with such compassion. He always picks her up from the floor, which is hard as Chris is slight, and she is heavy, having developed a large upper body. But he carries her in his arms everywhere whenever we are there. She loves it, and we wonder if it may be the only physical contact she receives.

"You know everybody goes to bed early Christine, because of having no light, so are you ready to wake everyone up?"

When we arrive we see candlelight around the curtain and no one is in bed. Instead, everyone is trying to comfort Gracia and she shrieks in delight on hearing the dogs barking and knows that it's the new missionary who has arrived. But she is distressed about something, her eyes swollen through crying. The family explain how Gracia has wept all day long, praying that the new missionary would arrive today to pray with her. Chris does his best to help, and we pray, and Gracia calms down. We wonder if she had been asking for some sign, and our arriving had been it. But she isn't willing to disclose the reason for her distress or the need for prayer.

As we are leaving, Gracia asks why we had travelled up so late. Until she asked, the animal had been forgotten and was still inside the car, because it didn't matter any more. Gracia insists on seeing it. She prods the animal and says that it has been dead for a very long time, and that it is well on the way to decomposing. We leave the cave and our mysterious wild animal responsible for an answered prayer. If God can use a Donkey, we reason, he can use a dead civet cat.

On the way back home Chris and I chat about how flat it can feel when we arrive back home after such unusual experiences because of having no one to share any of them with.

--oOo--

One day, we are thrilled to be invited to have regular meetings in some little shack, the house of Lolita. I thought my hair was the longest, the thickest, and the blackest, until I met Lolita. She is beautiful and her raven black hair is to her waist, curly, and as thick as a horse's tail. She is a gypsy mother of six, yet still only twenty-seven years old. I feel sorry for Lolita. She keeps food in her children's mouths by picking tomatoes in Palomares. Her husband lives a care-free life of selfishness and laziness. The squalid condition of their half built hovel is left in the hands of the older children, who care for the younger ones while Lolita walks all the way to work and back. As usual there are never any toilets wherever we go, and theirs is a rock down the yard. It is obvious that the little ones never make it that far. The smell and myriads of flies are overwhelming. Apart from the disruption of children in a meeting, there is always the battle of the flies, and sometimes I have wondered if they are demons in disguise. Whenever I am playing the choruses on my accordion they seem to attack me more than anyone else. It's impossible to knock them off my lips, nose, and face as I play. People just seem to put up with them.

I visit Lolita one day by myself, and find her new-born baby Maria, sick. I know the symptoms well. It is what Wesley had. Then Lolita tells me, that not too long ago, she lost a baby boy with the same symptoms, so she is now in a panic. She explains how the baby boy she lost, and the new baby girl, are the only two babies out of all of her children that she had been unable to suckle herself, and she wonders if there is a connection. I note the feeding bottle plastered in flies!

Lolita has started to respond to the things of the Lord, and also to the servants he has sent her way, which has eased some of the pain in her life. She has started to trust me. I explain to her how flies are a source of disease. I persuade her to have her only kitchen brought indoors; a rickety old cabinet standing outside in the burning sun near the 'rock' bathroom. I wash the cabinet down with my disinfectant from England. Then I spray the room with my precious fly spray until the flies are dropping by the hundreds. I then teach her how to sterilize feeding bottles. I encourage her to share all her worries with the Lord, and to treat Him as her new friend.

On my next visit Maria is well. Lolita is thrilled. She is pregnant again. Lolita gives birth to another baby girl, her eighth. She expresses her desire to me that she wants to break the essential tradition of naming each child after a relative. She tells me that although it will cause much trouble for her, she is going to name the baby after me!

As I gaze down into the tiny face of baby Cristina nestled in my arms, a stunning realization comes over me. That right out here, where no one visits, and where no one really knows where we are, or what we are doing, in a dirty, worthless place called Vera, the Lord is allowing me to make a difference in someone's life.

How I would love to share these blessings with someone. How I would love to be serving the Lord with other missionaries, all of us together, sharing the sorrows, and laughing together about the joys. How I would love to share the testimony with someone about the civet cat. How I would love someone to know about baby Maria. How I would love to be allowed to take some photographs to send to England, to show off baby Cristina.

How I would love people to see all this.

It could take faith… to work unnoticed.

"Are not five sparrows sold for two cents? Yet not one of them is forgotten before God." (Luke 12:6)

11

It Could Take Faith…
to lose a good reputation

Christine is changing. She is losing her identity.

In my country women are conservative, and dress sombre and traditional. Here too, the mode is drab. But I want to blend better with the gaudy types in cave ministry. A scripture in Matthew is so tempting, "He who has lost his life for my sake will find it."(Matthew 10:39)

Although Mom and Dad had spoiled me in so many ways, make-up had never been part of the goodies. Make-up was seriously discouraged, and only for the vain and unspiritual or those wanting to attract the wrong kind of attention. I had never as much as looked at a make-up counter or even had a desire to. If a person in the church was seen to be even lingering around a make-up counter, they were showing the early signs of backsliding, and would soon get a lecture. Jewellery was also considered to be an inward longing for the world. I had never seen Mom wear one piece, except for her thin 22ct gold wedding ring. A splatter of tasteful fine gold jewellery may be given the benefit of the doubt for a special occasion, but earrings were a different story. There was something about earrings that meant you were a Jezebel, and the same went for lipstick, nail polish, eye shadow, or rouge. They were all termed as the attire of a loose woman. Ours was a puritanical way of life.

My wedding was beautiful and lavish. Dad had already had the expense of my sisters' weddings, so I appreciated how he spared no expense for mine. I had the best photographers, the best cars, and an expensive reception with a sit-down meal. My wedding dress had been specially made for me. My older sister and I had driven two hours to Nottingham to choose the Nottingham lace that I – or perhaps she – wanted my dress to be made from. My headdress was made from real crystals from Beatties, the most expensive shop in Wolverhampton, and where I also bought my long trailing veil, with the Nottingham lace stitched around the edges. Yet, I was still a twenty year old bride with a shiny face. Make-up hadn't been a passing thought. My sisters wore make-up on my wedding day, but that was only to be expected from any backsliders.

--oOo--

The new role into which I am now slipping is against everything I have ever known, and I am quite aware of the problems it will present me with. Ours was an abstinence Christianity. As I paint my toenails for the first time, I know how family, friends, and relatives would be disappointed in me, which hurts more than losing my identity. I don't like to be the cause of disappointment to anyone.

My future respect and reputation as a missionary and wife of a minister depends on what I am allowing myself to become. After all, missionaries aren't supposed to be the ones who change, but the people they have gone to.

I feel like a teenager spreading colour over my lips for the very first time, as if handling a stick of dynamite, yet I am a grown woman, and the mother of three children. I had never realized until this moment just how much a reputation must have meant to me.

At Lolita's house one day she kindly offers to pierce my ears. I am asked so many times why I don't have my ears pierced. It is something strange to people, so I thought I had best get it done. I go to Lolita's for advice. She is thrilled and says she has the answer. She brings out a box, and gets from it a fat needle she keeps for the purpose of piercing the ears of newborn girls. She even has bits of wire available until I can get some earrings! My panic makes me feel stupid and feeble as I compare it to Lolita's hard life, seeing her hands covered in grime and wounds from plantation picking. But she laughs and laughs as I run off refusing to let her get near me, telling her I have changed my mind and will never have the courage to have my ears pierced after all. We both enjoy a time of joking about my fear of needles, bugs, heat and sunlight intolerance, and how I have to come to a place where there's loads of all four.

One day, Lolita surprises me by presenting me with a big pair of bright red plastic clip-on earrings. So with lipstick, tanned skin, and my long straight jet black hair, which Lolita has greased until it is plastered to my head and shines like glass; a new me has emerged. I look into a mirror and a complete stranger is looking back at me. But I am pleasantly surprised at how it has also made me feel more hidden, helping me feel a bit more confident.

I am directed to a lady seamstress who turns one of my garments into a gypsy-type skirt and blouse, and the part looks complete.

I can hardly take in that a call was going to change the missionary so dramatically. The results are making any conflicts over losing my identity worthwhile. I blend far better than I could have hoped, and it will feel liberating not to stand out and have all eyes fixed on me as if I have dropped from space which makes it hard for Chris to get attention in the caves while preaching. I have found an answer, the Apostle Paul encouraging me, "I have made myself a slave to all, that I may win more." (1 Corinthians 9:19). I wish I'd have become a slave sooner.

However, I am aware that I will be accepted by one culture, but will be dropped by my own. My image has been well hidden up to now, as there have been no visitors to carry back any reports, but there soon will be. Mail has arrived. As well as our parents, others are planning to come – close friends from back home.

How I had longed to see people, and craved English company. How I had ached to share some of the things the Lord was doing. But why couldn't they have come before I had changed my image, like the 'Missions Board' of our denomination had! One day, without any notification, the 'Missions Board' actually arrived at the Centro – especially to see us! They just suddenly turned up right out of the blue. Chris and I had been nothing less than stunned when we saw them all standing there!

The Executive and Missions Boards were the elite to us. At the Annual General Conferences, the youth would almost swoon if any of them happened to pass them by on the way to a meeting. We used to call them 'the untouchables.' They sat on the huge ballroom stage before thousands at the holiday camps where the conferences were held. So when the 'untouchables' suddenly appeared on our very doorstep at the Centro, it was the biggest shock ever. It was like a 'mirage'. So much so, that Chris literally jumped on seeing them, and I almost kissed the Missions Secretary to prove they weren't a mirage. There they were – actually in our mission house. But an even bigger shock was yet to come. They started to compliment us. They kept congratulating us on coming out alone, and on building a mission station all by ourselves. They kept looking around the Centro intrigued and talked about us being what real pioneer missionaries were all about. We were shocked and baffled, as they had been the very ones to deny our request to be sent out as their missionaries, and the ones who had said they couldn't offer us any 'official help', once they knew we would still be going to the mission-field.

So to see them arrive unannounced, and to hear them keep praising what we had done, was amazing. We just kept listening to what wonderful pioneering missionaries we were. Then the Missions Secretary said to Chris, "You have a real flair for missions Chris."

Then, of all things, they dropped an even bigger bombshell. They asked us if we would consider becoming their missionaries! They asked if we would consider Centro Cristiano being their missionary 'arm' in Spain! We were stunned. I felt a sudden rush of belonging. We were being noticed. Someone cared. They admired us again, like when we were 'Kris and Kristine – The Sunshine Evangelists.'

My mind went crazy about what it could mean. With our denomination involved with us here, we wouldn't be alone any more. Being back with our denomination again, would mean that we would be the headquarters for this entire region – and with a mission station at that. We'd have someone to share with about all the things I wanted to. We'd be of some importance. So I was stunned and taken aback when I heard Chris graciously thanking them, but explaining that since we had chosen a life of faith, we would have to continue as we were, as it would feel like turning our back on the path God had started us on. This was our last chance to be back in the fold again, and it had gone. I was so disappointed. But I suppose Chris was right.

How I must have unconsciously enjoyed the high opinion of my denomination. And how it probably showed when they had admired our little wonder, the Centro. The admiration had made my heart flutter for a while. So I dread now, what will be reported back about me after our friends have visited us and seen my change of image. I am tormented to think that my denomination could say how it was just as well Chris didn't accept the invitation to go back with them, as we hadn't been missionary material after all, because of his wife.

How will I explain to our friends, that I am still the same Christine they have known for years? Explanations will only sound like a pathetic excuse for something Christine wants to do. But I have realized something. That worldliness isn't to do with a particular dress code – what we had always been taught worldliness to be. Now, I see that worldliness is something more serious. It is making the world's current trend or value try to fit Christianity, no matter what the scripture says to the contrary.

I don't really cherish losing any more of my reputation than we already have over not being able to get into Cuevas. I would have liked our friends to go back admiring and approving of me, instead of cutting themselves off like they will need to do if not wanting to be seen as condoning sin. Maybe I can conceal my new image until the visitors have gone!

Losing a reputation is proving to be harder than I had expected, because it will seem to them, that I don't really love the Lord, or know the Lord as I once did, or like they do. We had been conditioned to show our Christianity, to parade it. There had to be an outward visible proof of how real someone was, by the identical way they spoke, and the identical way they dressed. But I am already realizing that the answer can't be to conceal my new image after all. My children, my young, innocent 'sheep' will note any hypocrisy. For their sake I can't risk putting on a different cloak because someone is coming to visit. The children need to see that wherever we are, or whoever we are with, that they only have one Mom or Dad.

I have to work out what this losing a life is actually all about, "…Whoever loses his life for my sake will find it…" How is a life lost? What life is then found? Does losing a life mean letting the Lord do what he wants with it, instead of what one would do with it one's self? Could losing a life be losing the approval, respect, and admiration of friends, yet be gaining something invisible to the human eye – the approval of God? It could take faith for me to do that, only having been accustomed to a display-type Christianity, as an indication of the reality within.

I never expected that coming to be a missionary was going to present *me*, the missionary, with all these spiritual challenges and choices. I thought missionaries came to change others.

But I haven't lost my reputation yet, not until they arrive. However, because I know the values we were brought up to adhere to, a reputation will be lost when I am seen.

I have lost my freedom, and now it will be my culture, my friends, my denomination. I have to admit how significant the good opinion of others must have been to me, and how it has taken coming here to reveal it.

I am going to get buried – and by the very ones who had elevated and held me in high esteem and by ones I need and love. I won't be top of that spiritual list any more. The real Christine is going to be hidden. Any struggles to exist on this mission-field, and any cravings to survive a life of faith, won't be seen. They will all be hidden beneath a pair of worthless plastic earrings, greased hair, lipstick, and a gaudy outfit. But I know dying to self will be wearing them.

How I wish I still didn't have this need to live up to what people expect. Why do I still long to be accepted, and for Christians to say good, and not bad about me? Is that pride? People will be going back to England saying, "Christine doesn't love the Lord as she once did."

I am going to lose all the benefits I had of being me, the admiration, the respect – the friendships.

Yet Jesus, "…emptied himself…" So He must have given up His rights? "…He humbled himself…" So He must have made Himself of no importance? He must have lowered Himself? So is losing a life all about humility? According to James 4:6, humility and pride are enemies, "God is opposed (against) to the proud, but gives grace to the humble."

But it's hard to be humble! I can hear those words in scripture about backsliders "The dog has returned to his vomit." As young people, we had held our head up high when that scripture was read out in a meeting. Backsliding was for others! Not for us! It was the ultimate sin and disloyalty to a God who had saved us. It was about people who hadn't really known the Lord in the first place. It was being weak.

I can just hear it, "Christine has backslidden on that mission-field. She mustn't have been as strong as we thought." I will always be a backslider. I won't be 'quite there' any more. I will have fallen from the ladder, and I don't know if I can stand the height of this fall, to let people think I'm not spiritual any more.

The visitors couldn't be arriving at a worse time – FIESTA-TIME! Each tiny village boasts their very own fiesta, each at a different time of the year, and each dedicated to their particular saint. A fiesta is one activity encouraged and approved by the State.

Repressed talents are let loose for four days of the year. There is an atmosphere of excitement and expectation. For months on end, the women's dedication to needlework is intriguing. All moms use every spare second, in between fetching water, feeding animals and babies, and scrubbing clothes, to stitch frill upon frill, petticoat upon petticoat, lace, ribbons, and umpteen buttonholes, right into the early hours. It seems like a competition to see who will make their little girl the best model on a catwalk with the most unique of frocks, with not a sewing pattern in sight. These people may be repressed, but are not unintelligent.

The motivation can be tasted. A mass of gaudy colours brighten up ugly untidy streets, in the form of balloons, old streamers, worn flags, flowers, and ribbons. A flurry of action is so refreshing in such a listless oppressed place.

They string up palm tree branches across crumbling buildings, and thread them through with big old fashioned bulbs. Rickety carts appear full of odd treats such as pipas, bits of pork fat, dry salted fish, fried corn, snails, and monkey nuts. It all excites Calvin, yet I can imagine what children back in England would say if they were presented with such 'exciting' treats at a fairground. There is a constant sound of the cracking of pipas; the shells pile up on the floor which everyone trails through. A pipa shell is cracked open with the teeth to let the seed pop out. We can't master it. Just like alcachofas, everything is a lot of trouble for a little morsel, yet the happiness on everybody's face makes up for simplicity and lack.

The source of happiness and amusement are children. They proudly parade their youngsters in beautiful Flamenco dresses, and hand crochet matching lace shawls, in a bid to get the widest smile and biggest nod of approval as they walk their girls up the same grotty street and back down again – in the most elegant of shoes. They don't notice dust, potholes, pipa and monkey nut shells. The men walk in front, and women and children trail behind arm in arm chatting into the early hours of the morning, to make their fiesta last as long as they possibly can. They discuss one topic – the exact amount of hours it took to stitch a buttonhole, or frill, and the exact time each night they eventually dropped into bed.

The battered sets of bumper cars and other rides arrive via gypsies. Calvin's eyes are popping out with glee, to see so much happening.

I suddenly remember how I haven't told Calvin that the visitors think fun fairs sinful. Now it's too late; the visitors have arrived and Calvin is jumping up and down for joy all ready to go.

I know our friends will find it unspeakable to go anywhere near a fiesta, and will want to know why we, the missionaries do, and especially when they know it is about the celebration of 'Saints'. They will think that missionaries should define the 'dos and don'ts'. They have come to be inspired by us! To learn from us, the spiritual ones who left all for the sake of the gospel! For our friends to walk around a noisy street, and beer being served into the early hours, is a big 'don't'. It will seem as if it is they who are setting the example when it should be us. They won't understand because it isn't them living in a completely dull, boring, monotonous place with no television, no telephone, no radio, no magazines, no newspapers, no electricity, no water, no meat, no life; and freedom for just one week out of fifty-two.

This fiesta will be my funeral, the place where the dirt will be thrown over me. I know because it was who we were once.

The fiesta is in full swing when our visitors get out of the car. The throbbing hot crowded streets are buzzing with all the noisy silly things that are enjoyed so much by simple suppressed peasant folk for one week a year. Even the mere sight of bottles of wine lined up along the tables, which make a persecuted oppressed race happy, joyful, and forgetful, for four days of the year, will be unacceptable to our friends.

To us, it is just something interesting and peculiar to watch, as well as the need to mix, get known, and distribute invitations. But I am unnerved by the fiesta for other reasons. It is hard watching grown ups derive pleasure from such childish activities. Calvin is overwhelmed by it all, but he is only a little boy. The uniformity of satisfaction is an image of restriction; growth has been stunted. They gain the exact same pleasure from the exact same things as fifty years earlier, and the clues are ancient tatty jaded streamers, crumpled balloons, faded flowers, and rickety broken chairs and tables. They are things that should only be thrilling children.

They are lives which have been robbed by one man of the very thing God had created human beings to have – freedom and choice. Franco owns each person. He owns all the brains in Spain, reminding me of a scripture, "The thief comes only to steal" (John 10:10). The urges God had created man to have, to be productive, attain, and grow, are only stimulated once a year for these deprived villagers. It is no wonder the intense dedication to a fiesta, when they taste free will for a while.

As we walk around the shabby noisy fairground, with its distorted deafening off-key brass band, ring-throw, darts, and pop-guns, I see how people are suffering through brain restriction.

I pray a lot for the freedom of these people, the gift of freedom which the Maker fashioned each human being to have. To be able to choose, accomplish, achieve, and enjoy the rewards good choices bring, just as in my own country. "It is He who is giving you the power to make wealth" (Deuteronomy 8:18).

According to the parable of the talents, which were given according to the people's abilities, if freedom ever does come to this country, some will gain wealth, some not – according to abilities. But as in other free countries, those with abilities will be a provision for those with none "For you always have the poor with you" (Mark 14:7).

--oOo--

My burial has started. I can sense disapproval that our children are being brought up wrong. Calvin's beaming face on the bumper cars makes up for the stinging remark by Matthew who won't even get out of the car to walk around the fiesta stating pompously, "I was delivered from all of that!"

I had so looked forward to enjoying our first visitors. I don't blame them for anything. It was us in the past. We had all been brought up to have the same convictions, the same dress code, the same taste in music, even to the wearing of the same hats in a service – if we wanted to be seen as holy that is. A fiesta has shown me, that a Creator who chose to make every snowflake, star, and blade of grass different, would surely make the most important of his creations distinct. A fiesta has given me a sudden distaste for duplicates unless born a twin.

With my reputation lost, I have already found my first something, because I have learned two new lessons. The first is on freedom and choice, and the second is on judging and passing sentence on others. "For who are you to judge the servant of another" (Rom 14:4).

As we are about to enter a cave, I know that our friends won't even pretend to sip from the stone water jar that will be passed around. They will have to visibly object when they discover it contains wine not water, to protect their reputation. That is their choice. Choice has now become valuable to me since living where there is none. I now understand that this is their conviction, and this is our call, not theirs. But I know that their choice, convictions, and preferences, are expected to be everyone's. When they see us sip from the bottle, I know that if my red toenails hadn't quite buried me deep enough, this one certainly will. It will be the passing of a sentence and burial all in one go – good and deep.

With a disdainful look at Chris and me as we sip from the stone jar, the funeral is over. As well as earrings and lipstick, the worst transgression of all, is that we drink! Drinking is the worst sin ever to them, and the one that will be carried back to spread like fire back home, embarrassing our Moms, and making their missionary babies – sinners. My Mom, her church, and our denomination, are so opposed to drinking, they only have grape juice in the churches for Communion. The very first thing any new convert is told to give up, is drinking.

I feel a sudden sense of loss, because the life I have always known has well and truly gone. We are now truly alone in the life we have been called to. I will never be an esteemed missionary, like those I had always admired. I will be the weak one who allowed others to influence me instead of the other way around. I hope the life I am going to find is a good one. I suddenly feel a sense of relief that the turmoil is over. A reputation takes too much pride to hold on to.

It is the disappointment on the faces of the cave dwellers; a people avoided and rejected in life, which I will never forget. It makes me realize that our English friends have lost their reputation too! But, they have lost it with the wrong people. I wondered how many times we had lived to impress the wrong people. "And he must have a good reputation to those *outside* the Church" (1 Timothy 3:7). It seems it must be too hard to have one *inside* the church.

For months the cave dwellers had been looking forward to the visit of our Christian friends. The meagre hospitality they had so happily prepared had been rejected. They didn't feel good enough for 'posh' English visitors. The cave dwellers were used to rejection, but had thought we were different, and thought they were going to experience what acceptance felt like.

Having watched this race live out the decisions, preferences, tastes, and convictions of one person, has made me determined never to do the same. I will only lose my life to One. My 'Dictator' will only be the One who "made Himself of no reputation."

Any remaining pangs of doubt about a reputation are soothed away as I see how God can be deprived of the pleasure of being 'Lord' in the lives of His children, all because of the desire for the high opinion of a fellow Christian. The chorus, "He is Lord," comes to mind, and I don't ever want it to be for me: 'they' 'she' 'he' are Lord.'

I suddenly see the futility of God working on someone if they only have the courage to live by the convictions of another, because of not wanting to be seen as unspiritual. "For they loved the approval of men rather than the approval of God" (James 12:43). Why should God acquire identical offspring, when He had chosen to make each distinct?

I am pleased that my reputation has flown all the way back to England and that it is now in some little scruffy Moorish street, with those outside the church.

No one would have guessed that day that the Mom with the big earrings, bright lipstick, and gaudy clothing, laughing at her son on the bumper cars, was the missionary who had lost something which had been so precious to her – a reputation within the church.

I am grateful for a fiesta because as well as my reputation, I have also discovered that I have lost something else. I have lost a burden. A burden I was completely unaware of having until the fiesta – one of not needing to prove to anyone, how much I love or know the Lord, or my level of spirituality.

After reading Matthew 11:18, 19, it seems it may be impossible to have a reputation inside the church anyway, as if John or Jesus couldn't, who could?

"For John came neither eating or drinking, and they say, 'He has a demon!'"

"The son of man came eating and drinking, and they say, 'Behold, a gluttonous man and a drunkard…'"

It could take faith… to lose a good reputation.

12

It Could Take Faith...
to replace family relationships

Mom and Dad have arrived – their cases bulging with food, in addition to plastic bags of more food. Obviously Mom has no intention of trying out any local delicacies. She has brought enough sustenance to last their entire visit. I drool at the sight of tins of red salmon, tins of stewed steak, custard creams, cheddar cheese, and plenty of Mom's 'best butter.' We don't understand how they have been able to lift their cases.

Clothes aren't Mom's priority. Dad complains how his new shirts have been rolled around food. "I told Flossy" he says, "that we won't have enough clothes because of all this food, but she insisted we would be more miserable without food than clothes." Then Mom begins to throw away all their half eaten sandwiches from the journey – red salmon and cucumber, on soft white bread with best butter. I just stop her in time. She watches in disbelief as I polish them all off. It's a pity how the English are unaware at how blessed they are.

Mom is a sweet-natured person, but more often than not is preoccupied with the troubles of the world. She knows every sad story, because of a compassionate heart. Mom is a spiritual woman, and loves and serves the Lord with all her heart. She dotes on children, and caters to their every whim. It has hurt me to see how Mom and Dad have been deprived of their grandchildren. Mom is a great cook, and makes delicious apple pies. Whenever Chris came from Fleetwood to the Midlands to visit me, he always looked forward to Mom's extravagant roast dinners piled high with the best silverside roast beef. Chris came from a family of not so plenty.

My Mom had never thought to bring gravy mix in her case – but as we haven't found any meat fit for human consumption as yet, it doesn't matter. We were offered a 'tappa' at someone's house once, and I was horrified later when we found out that we had eaten goat meat!

Chris's Mum's packing is a different cup of tea. Her case is overflowing with dresses she has made herself especially for this visit. She hasn't brought one item of food – apart from chocolates for the children. Mum has a great figure, with a nipped-in waist, and wears high-heeled shoes all day every day. She is fashion conscious and loves to discuss clothes. Mum has always put curlers in her hair every single night to sleep in. The very first thing she does in a morning is pull them out, and lacquer her hair in place for the day. The first thing my Mom does in a morning is put the kettle on to make a cup of tea.

I had learned so much from Chris's Mum regarding ministry. I saw her put ministry before anything and everything, including her children. She never felt it was detrimental that they attend Church several times on Sunday, and several times during the week.

Mum's weakness is clothes, and especially hats. Mum is unpacking, and we have to be Winifred's audience. She keeps changing from one dress to another, proudly parading each one to show off her sewing skills, and to ask us to choose which is the prettiest for an occasion. She doesn't realize yet, that she has arrived at a place where there is no 'occasion,' and that it isn't like holidaying in other places. She is going to look and feel out of place dressed up in this poverty-stricken place. "I know there won't be enough time to wear all of the dresses," she says, "but I just couldn't decide which one to leave behind, so had to bring them all." Chris's Mum would have been in her element with all the mothers preparing for a fiesta, with her expert stitching talents. The first thing Mum did when I went to see Chris for the very first time in Fleetwood, was to whip out a tape measure and measure me up for a skirt. She and Chris's sister had it run up within minutes. I have a vivid picture of that pink cotton skirt with huge lilac flowers all over it. Mum is hat crazy, and on that first visit to Fleetwood she wanted to see my hats as soon as I arrived. She hadn't been too impressed, saying they were far too small. Mum's hats were something else. Like me, Mum is a good knitter. We can click our needles for hours. We have knitted our own dresses and suits. In England I had knitted Calvin's entire wardrobe, from jumpers to full sailor suits with matching sailor hats.

My Mom is shocked to see how her youngest spoiled daughter is living, and above all what she is eating, making justified her decision to bring food rather than clothes. She tells Dad, "See Bill! I told you food would be more important to us than clothes."

Mom and Dad can't wait to look after the children, while Winifred can't wait to get her face up to the sun, and eat oranges. If there is one thing we do have an abundance of, as well as bread, it is oranges, the likes of which my mum-in-law can't get enough of.

Chris and I have decided to go to a city for our first time out together, never having been to one as yet. We want to see the first new 'walk-around' store that has opened in Murcia that everyone is talking about even here hours away. It is called 'El Corte Ingles.'

My Dad faithfully promises that while we are away, he will not move from hovering over Cherry for the whole time we are away on seeing the problem with flies, and especially after Mom and Dad get to know about Wesley's illness. "I promise, not one fly will be allowed to land anywhere near her," he says. "Mom will do the cooking and I will watch the baby." I dread Mom and Dad going to the caves if they think the flies around here are bad.

We start out for the city early one morning before the sun is up to scorch us to death. But I can hardly enjoy the journey, not being able to get my mind off the children even for a day, not having been parted from them for a moment in so long. I am so glad, that faith was keeping them.

Although Mom has only been away from home for a few days, she is already craving a cake, the only thing that had been impossible for her to pack. She cannot believe she is in a 'cakeless' country. So Mom's strict order from the city, is to bring her back a cream cake in the hope they have some.

Mom and Dad have another job to do for us while we are away; look after our animals. We now own chickens, rabbits, geese and even – a goat. Although Chris still insists that God meets needs through a postman, he had kept his word and is prepared for any possibility of more postal strikes. So we are missionaries and farmers. Chris has also tried growing potatoes and other vegetables, but due to the salty ground, has had no success. So apart from the time it takes to shop from one 'curtain' shop to another, and wash in trenches, we now have to find time to feed and look after animals.

When Chris bought the goat, we couldn't understand how we could afford one as it seemed rather cheap. Goat milk still unnerves me. I would have preferred a cow. We soon discovered the reason we could afford the goat. On Chris's first attempt to milk it, the children stood around excited with the container ready to catch the milk. But instead of the milk going into the container, it shot directly into Chris's eye. The goat was a damaged goat and the milk came out of a hole at the side instead of the normal place. We complained to the goatherd, and he had the goat back, returned our money, and apologized.

It wasn't long before we realized that the animals wouldn't sustain us after all – apart from eggs, because the children have turned them all into pets. One of our ducks acquires a broken leg, so my Dad decides he will make it a splint. But the splint sends the duck's leg flying upwards sticking straight up in the air. Chris says, "I wish everyone would get saved that quickly."

Calvin and Wesley are having great fun with the animals each day with their Nanny and Granddad, feeding and playing with the rabbits, while 'Ya Ya' – Mum's affectionate name for grandma – roasts herself to a crisp surrounded by orange peel.

There are only a few remarks from Mom and Dad about my painted toenails. They seem too sad at how I wash in a trench, and amazed how I've mastered the language, and let strangers plonk wet, strange smelling kisses on both sides of my face. But the bigger shock to Mom is seeing me eat tomatoes, carrots, and cucumbers, and how I can cook peculiar food. So my appearance isn't too much of an issue, except for one thing; Mom is preoccupied what her church and friends will think when they know. I haven't the heart to tell her it is too late. Mom is also extremely disappointed with Chris on finding out about the offer from our denomination to bring our ministry back into it.

Although I had been longing to hear all the happenings of mine and Chris's family, I had never expected to find it so painful. It dawns on me how we aren't part of the family's life any more. Each time Mom and Dad and Chris's Mum talk about them, it just confirms that fact. Until our parents arrived, I'd never thought about everybody's lives just continuing normally without us, and how people move on, adjusting to us not being around. We can see how we are losing track of each other's news.

Trying to keep in touch by telephone has proved a waste of time. We have to book the call days ahead from the one and only ancient phone office in Garrucha. Then when we arrive to make the call, it has more than likely been forgotten and has to be re-booked. Whenever we are successful, the line is so crackly, we all end up screaming to each other. The exorbitant cost has never been worth the frustration. I have to accept that living here means oblivion.

As our parents unwittingly show us photographs of all the things they have been doing with the families, I don't like that we are the only ones not in family photographs any more, and that they are the ones who still have our Moms around, all together as a family. Chris has a very big Christian family, all living within walking distance of each other in Fleetwood. In my view it had always been an ideal way of life.

I am thrilled to see our parents, but the visit is making too clear that we will eventually lose family relationships.

In the city, I actually find a cream cake for Mom, and it looks delicious. Chris and I are thrilled to find proper milk, eggs in a carton like in England, and a chicken without its feathers, crinkly neck, head, and claws on – but Mom hadn't brought gravy mix. Even the city folk are in awe of the first 'walk-around shop'; a place where it is cool. We decide we will come to it a couple of times a year. A six hour return journey going around mountains in a sweltering car to a city, hadn't been a priority due to our ministry being a travelling one. But we work out that if we left our house at around six o'clock in a morning, before the sun burned us alive in the car, we could be there for opening time and have a few hours in the cool. Our parents being with us is a reminder of how cut off we are living. Our decision to go to the city occasionally had really cheered us up.

When Mom sees the cake I have brought her back from El Corte Ingles, she treats it like a baby, even with respect. She says she is going to wait until tea-time to have it with her cup of tea. I realize how much the English like their routine. I am intrigued as I watch all the things that had bothered me, bothering them.

Our parents cannot believe how we find our way from one cave to another. A worried Winifred pipes up, "Everywhere looks the same Christopher. You will never find your way back – will you?" But when Chris does, there is huge relief, and Chris is the hero.

My Mom is fascinated by the beautiful young women, and amazed on seeing them chaperoned. But, Mom is far from fascinated with the cake. She chokes and splutters it out. "It's nothing more than sawdust, plastic pastry, and plastic cream Christine."

Apart from other things, Mom is finding particularly difficult the kissing of strangers on both sides of her cheeks when introduced. She feels extremely embarrassed by it, and blushes – more so, when two more kisses are repeated on saying goodbye, even if the person has only just had time to say 'Hola' (hello). It is four kisses in a row. Mom is now dreading going anywhere because of how awkward and uncomfortable it makes her feel. She always forgets it is going to happen a second time on saying goodbye. So when she is walking away, she is firmly grabbed, her cheeks sucked more severely as a kind of reminder that we do this twice over. She is also overwhelmed by the strong smell of what they have been eating which has to stay on her face until she can get to wash it off. The smell is the little pink thing Pepe loved, 'ajo' – garlic.

Although my Mom absolutely lived for her children, we hadn't been brought up touchy, or kissy. As far as Mom's children were concerned, nothing was ever too much trouble. As with Spaniards, a child's needs came before anything with Mom. She made any sacrifice. It was just that we didn't make feelings visible. In the West Midlands, families didn't show emotion full stop. That's why 'Midlanders' were termed as 'cold'. Feelings were things to be kept to one's self. It would embarrass if emotions were seen. I realized how different we were, when I visited Chris for the first time in Fleetwood. I was so surprised at how they kissed each other goodnight when going to bed – and right on the lips. It was something so new to me.

So, for Mom to be kissed by absolute strangers is almost rude. So she asks me a favour, "Christine, can you explain to them that we English aren't used to being kissed by people we have never met, and that we only shake hands?"

I laugh and tell her, "No Mom, I can't. This isn't England, and this is shaking hands to them. How would you feel if they came to England and they asked you to tell your friends not to shake their hand as they don't like touching the hands of strangers?" She understands but still doesn't feel that four wet, garlicky kisses, is very polite on a stranger's face.

It all becomes so real to me having Mom here, how patient God is to care enough to change someone instead of dismissing them. I had been brought up in a Christian home, and hadn't had much experience in needing to change.

I was converted at the age of twelve. It had happened one dark Saturday evening. My friend Val and I were in The Straits, Lower Gornal, and were being chased by a man. The horrid man was big and gaining on us. I was so terrified I spontaneously cried out loud to the Lord, "Please rescue us, and my life will be yours for ever and ever." I wondered if my friend would think me mad. She knew me as being quiet, now she hears me shouting in the street something to someone who isn't there. But we were suddenly aware of silence, and we fell to the floor too breathless to even comment.

The next night, at my Dad's Church – a little wooden hut in a field in Coseley, my Dad gave an altar call after his message. I had never told Mom or Dad what had happened to Val and me, but at twelve years of age I felt to walk to the front with friends; daughters of people in the Church. We all knelt down and made a decision to follow the Lord. There was Kay, Eunice, Norma, Janet, and me. Even at such a young age, I felt something had happened. After that, the five of us all started to dress alike and looked like quintuplets whenever we went to the Annual denominational Conference. We started to sing together, and then we arranged the annual anniversaries at Dad's church, and had all the children dress in white. For the first time after the conversion, I gained courage at school. I had been too shy to be open about my Dad being a pastor, and that I went to Church, as I was already being bullied by some awful girls who would wait outside the school gates to punch me. It was an all girls' school, and how I hated it. But after the conversion, I had the courage to witness at school, and various girls started coming to Dad's church, and started to receive the Lord. From then on, I had back up at school.

However, even though I have seen how God has taken the trouble to re-mould me here on this mission-field, we all know there is one thing in particular that none of us will ever adapt to or get used to here, and will never want to. It is our shock and disbelief at the cruelty to animals. We are afraid to take our parents to the little market. Meat is more available, if you buy it alive that is. It isn't served from counters, but cages. No fridges are necessary, as unsold 'meat' is just brought back in its cage for next market day. We are the only squeamish ones around. At times, we are desperate for meat, but we draw the line at choosing it before it is dead, or watching a rabbit's neck being broken, or a chicken's throat cut right in front of us. And as for plucking chicken feathers, and chopping off crinkly yellow feet!

I cried for days after seeing two baby goats with all fours tied together, and held upside down as their owner walked along while the goats' noses were being scraped along a filthy floor, leaving a trail of blood. When I pointed out to the man that he wasn't holding the goats high enough, it left him bewildered at how anyone could be crying over a goat. He ended up trying to be of comfort to *me,* instead of dealing with the reason I was upset.

I am glad however, that our children will learn some good things from this country. The elderly aren't discarded, they are treated with respect whatever their great age. They are never left to fend alone, but are cared for, and given dignified jobs of chaperone or baby sitter. Even if too infirm to walk, the courting couple or babies will be taken to them.

--oOo--

Our parents' visit is far too short. The lonely journey back from the airport is a sad and silent one.

As I walk through the field where Mom had walked, and see one of her chocolate wrappers, I know it will be such a long time before we will see them again. I still loathe this isolation.

We need more visitors, but several who came hated such remoteness, they left after two days, apologizing but headed for some resort. It was disappointing for Calvin and Wesley having got excited about being with visitors for two weeks.

In our melancholy mood about our parents and families, we decide to go to see Gracia. She is delighted as they had been patiently waiting to present the children with something special. "They are the biggest eggs our geese have produced yet," says Gracia, "and we have been saving them for the missionary children." Then to our surprise, they begin to load up the car boot with oranges, lemons, potatoes, cabbage, milk, cheese, eggs, figs, almonds, and wine. They tell us, "We have no money, but we want to bless our missionaries with what we have, because they faithfully climb this mountain every week to teach the Bible." The timing couldn't be more perfect.

Then they ask us to close our eyes, saying they have the real surprise for us. I have a dislike of surprises, and especially here. When we are told to open our eyes – there in front of us is our civet cat! Its dainty feet are perched on a piece of natural, unpolished wood, head upright, bushy striped tail high, its glassy eyes stunning.

Gracia and her brother explain what had happened the night we had left the animal with them. Gracia's brother only wanted to experiment taxidermy on it, needing to practise on a decomposing animal. However, Gracia convinced her brother that if they stayed up throughout that whole night it could be preserved. They'd had an argument about it, but in the end her brother relented and agreed to help his sister try and save it.

They explained how baffling it had been that there was no indication of the cause of the animal's death. They said that the odour had been the worst smell ever, and were convinced each passing hour that it was impossible to finish the job. Family members had gone searching to friend's houses for two glass beads to replace the eyes, and had found two with a black spot in the centre. They look like its real eyes. Gracia's brother explained how he had only ever watched someone doing taxidermy once. He is so excited and proud of his efforts as he presents it to us, his face beaming, waiting for our reaction. The cat is perfect. It is beautiful. It is ours. It will be a reminder of an answered prayer.

With our vehicle filled with the produce, and the civet cat perched on my lap, we start back home. The children each cradle their huge duck-egg, shouting at their Dad at every bump or swerve.

I am in the process of accepting that family relationships will fizzle. There isn't any contact, or any way for them to be kept. I think about Jesus when He said – that those who weren't His family, could be. "Anyone who does my will, is my brother, father, sister, mother." I know Jesus wasn't saying that family wasn't important, but I believe He can make up for the lack of any.

We are alone. We don't have any family around any more. These people, to whom God has sent us, will have to start replacing family relationships. These people will have to be our children's aunts, uncles, and cousins.

"Your people shall be my people." (Ruth 1:16)

It could take faith… to replace family relationships.

13

It Could Take Faith...
to believe he has a plan

I can't believe it!

The possibility of this happening to me had never crossed my mind. I hadn't expected, hoped, or thought of it. I hadnt even prayed about it.

All I had ever seen of America had been from films on TV in England. Now, I will be seeing the place for real! It's true. All of us have been invited to go to America as a family. Chris had been there already, just once. It had been nothing less than outstanding how he had got to go. It all started one Sunday when Chris was preaching in Rotherham Yorkshire.

After the service, an American gentleman introduced himself to Chris as Mr Reds Fingado. Chris was taken aback by the strong American accent in a northern town, and also by his immaculate appearance. Meeting an American in England was unheard of for us. We knew none. Mr Fingado said he was from New York, and Chris was baffled what a clean cut sharp New Yorker would be doing in a rather neglected town in Yorkshire.

Mr Fingado expressed how much he had enjoyed Chris's message and testimony, so said he would be writing to his church 'Calvary Temple,' in New York, recommending that his Pastor, The Rev. Daniel Mercaldo invite him to speak at his Church! Chris was flattered that he had blessed an American of all people, and thanked him for the compliment. But Chris never dreamt for one moment, that Mr Fingado really did come from this church in New York. He thought he'd probably just visited it at some time. Neither could Chris believe someone could have any influence on a New York Pastor to invite someone to preach who he had never met or heard of. So Chris just thought Mr Fingado was probably trying to impress, because of the English view that Americans were big-headed and boasters. However, not long afterwards, an envelope dropped through our letter-box, bearing a NEW YORK postmark. The New York postmark was like magic to our eyes, and even our postman was nosey to know what a letter from New York could be about. Chris and I were stunned that Mr Fingado was not only who he said he was, but had been true to his word, and had actually done what he said would do. Chris felt terrible for having doubted him.

Without hesitation, Chris rushed to a travel agent to enquire about aeroplane fares and flights to New York. But he returned downcast. "It's like needing an air-fare to the moon," he said. "Even your Dad would think it too much Christine."

We resigned ourselves to the fact that there was no possibility of Chris accepting the invitation. It had only been an invitation. There was no fare, or help to get there. But just the invitation, on thick embossed writing paper, with raised letters that read 'Calvary Temple' had tickled us pink, and I put it in our keepsake box.

Sometimes we would get out the letter and matching envelope just to feel its texture and to read Chris's name on a New York letterhead from Calvary Temple. We'd discuss how we would be able to prove to our children one day that their dad, at just twenty-five years of age, was personally invited to preach in New York!

We didn't know anyone who had been to America. America was one of those places people would promise to treat themselves if they were ever left something in a will, or if ever they won lots of money. Time passed, and the invitation was behind us.

When our dormer bungalow had sold in Golborne, we went to stay with Chris's Mum in Fleetwood for a little while, being only a short drive away from Golborne, and Mum being recently widowed. It was just until we went to my Mom's in the Midlands where I would have the baby before leaving for the mission-field.

While we were staying with Chris's Mum, we decided to visit my Mom and Dad in the Midlands for a weekend to arrange the hospital details for the birth of our second child. On the Sunday morning we attended Mom's church at Upper Gornal. Chris wasn't the preacher. As we sat listening to the preacher, the American invitation popped into my mind. I felt to take hold of Chris's hand and whisper in his ear. "Chris, let's agree, let's believe, and let's ask the Lord if He would supply that plane ticket for you to be able to go to New York."

Chris was taken aback. We couldn't keep whispering to each other during a service, so we started to scribble notes to each other on a scrap of paper from my Bible. Chris scribbles, "So are you saying that you wouldn't mind me going all that way to USA leaving you all alone at such a crucial time, when you are weeks away from giving birth?"

I scribbled back, "No. I would only be too thrilled for you to go, and especially so if the Lord supplied the fare."

As the speaker was closing in prayer, Chris and I squeezed each other's hand, and whispered our own private prayer together, about what we had discussed via a scrap of paper. We decided that Chris would reply to Pastor Mercaldo and say that it was possible to accept his invitation after all.

As we were leaving the service and got to the foyer, two gentle quaint ladies stopped to talk to us. Being polite and unassuming, one of them stepped aside for the other to speak first. She discreetly pushed an envelope into Chris's hand whispering, "The Lord has laid it on my heart, just this morning, to give you this gift." Then the other lady came forward and said the same thing. They were the Holder sisters, and were missionaries in Israel.

When we got into the car and out of sight, Chris feverishly tore open the two envelopes. There were two cheques, one from each of them, and the two cheques totalled up the exact amount that Chris had priced at the travel agent, for the one-way plane ticket to New York.

Chris exclaimed, "I CAN'T BELIEVE IT LOVE! I'M GOING TO NEW YORK!" We both cried, hugging each other.

No one in the meeting could have known about the secret prayer we had whispered to each other as the minister closed the service. No one there knew about an invitation to New York. But then, on the way back to Fleetwood, Chris and I wondered if the scrap of paper on which we had been scribbling to each other had fallen out of our Bible on the floor of the church, and that someone had read it. We stopped the car to quickly go through our pockets and our Bibles. The notes were still in our possession.

"Sweetheart, no one will really believe that little old Chris Smith, is really going to preach in New York."

He was right. No one did. There were peals of laughter, thinking Chris was cracking jokes as usual.

"Preach in America!?" laughed his sister-in-law. Then, pointing her finger at her little fresh-faced brother-in-law, she turned to me, as if it was one of Chris's jokes, and said, "Who? Him? Him?" I was startled, but then I realized – that to her – Chris was just her little mischievous brother-in-law, and the younger of the two preacher brothers in the family.

The words New York had been magic to everybody we mentioned it to. There were gasps at the mention of going to AMERICA. Through Chris's invitation, we had unwittingly discovered what every preacher craved to do, which was to receive a proper written invitation to preach in America, and Chris had.

After everyone realized it wasn't a joke, and that Chris really was going to preach in New York, I started to identify with Joseph and his coat of many colours. I wondered if he ever felt like leaving the coat at home some days! But after we had excitedly told everyone, and after everyone eventually believed us, the travel agent refused to sell Chris a ticket! They told him they were not allowed to.

We felt so stupid. "Imagine Chris, you can't go now. We have even said how the Lord had provided the fare!" We were wishing more than ever we had kept it all to ourselves.

We started to think we may have it wrong, and that the two cheques from the Holder sisters had just been ministry gifts. The people at Mom's church did know we were going to be missionaries. We reasoned that although the Holder sisters didn't say what the money was for, it was probably

165

a missionary gift, and may not have been given had they known it was going to be used for a ticket to New York.

Chris still went back to the travel agent to enquire further the reason they wouldn't sell him a ticket. They told him they weren't allowed to sell one-way tickets to America without a visa. They advised Chris he should make an appointment for an interview at the American Embassy in London. But they made it clear how difficult it was to get a visa to America even with a return fare, let alone with only a one-way ticket, and that was why they hadn't mentioned an interview before. Then the travel agent asked Chris, "Why are you only wanting a one-way ticket anyway Mr Smith? All our customers buy return tickets. Don't you intend to come back?" Chris knew the travel girl wouldn't understand if he told her that he only had enough money for a one-way ticket. All our money was spoken for. Every penny had already been changed into foreign currencies.

Chris prepared for a fourteen hour return journey to London. Chris's Mom and I were praying for him all through the exact time of the appointment.

The American lady behind the embassy desk was brusque and unpleasant, and Chris wondered how he would cope with such arrogant Americans if he did get a visa. She bombarded him with a string of questions. "How much money do you have to take with you? Why are you going? Why are you only buying a one-way ticket sir? Can you prove to me that you will be returning? Why don't you have a home in England to return to? Are you trying to stay?"

To cover up that he had no money to take, Chris replied, "I really don't think that the amount of money I have, or how much I am taking, is any of your business."

This made the Embassy lady very cross. She answered sharply, "Oh, but it IS my business sir, because it is me who has power to let you go, and it is me who has the power to refuse your application." When Chris realized who he had been speaking with, and just how serious an interview was, and how serious every visa application was taken and how unwise and flippant he'd been – he was stunned. He knew right there on the spot that he'd blown his chances, and that everything she was writing down, was an official refusal.

As the travel agent suggested, Chris had even taken the invitation with him, as proof he had received one. The Lord had even met the need with the fare, yet through his own silly fault, he wasn't going to preach in New York after all.

Everything was against it. The worst thing of all was that he didn't have an English home address any more, the absolute proof the American Embassy insists on to prove a visitor will return.

So Chris could hardly believe his ears, when he heard the woman snap, "OK Mr Smith, I am going to give you a visa! But give me all the details of who you are going to be staying with, and what you will be doing. I am going to give you just fourteen days sir. It is in your interest that you do not try to stay for longer."

I'd never seen a Jumbo Jet in my life. When his Mom and I spotted Chris's face pressed at the little window as the huge monster taxied away, tears welled up in my eyes as we stood waving frantically on the spectators' balcony. We didn't want to tell his Mom that he hadn't got a return ticket, and only one date to preach, so she was baffled at my concern. I prayed quietly, "Please Lord, bless him. Please let the Church like him, and please supply his fare home."

Our baby was due on twenty-fifth of October 1970, and Chris was off to New York, in September 1970 for two weeks. I hadn't told Chris just how frightened I really was being left without him, and just how poorly I felt. I really felt in that meeting at Upper Gornal, that the Lord wanted him to go to New York, and even more so after the Lord had met the need for the fare after we'd prayed. But I knew he wouldn't have gone if he had thought that I was worried in any way.

Chris's Mum and I left the airport, having stayed until the plane couldn't be seen any longer. All the way back to Mum's flat, she chattered on about what an incredible thing was happening for her youngest son. She was so proud of him.

The two weeks Chris was away in New York dragged. I was terrified he wouldn't be back for the birth if I started labour early. I decided I would have to fill my time and thoughts somehow. Mum lived in a small flat above Chris's brother's house, after Stanley, Chris's dad, had passed away. Mum played the piano, but she didn't have one in her little flat for me to occupy my time. There wasn't much to do in a tiny flat in blustery Fleetwood. One day Calvin and I had a little walk around Fleetwood. We found ourselves in a back street where there was a tiny shop, and the only thing in the window, was a large tapestry picture of a Spanish Flamenco lady. I was so taken aback on seeing a big picture of a Spanish Flamenco dancer in a tiny back street shop in Fleetwood, I bought it. My large pregnant tummy acted as my table as I couldn't afford the frame the shop lady advised I needed to work on for such a large tapestry with such a large tummy. I sewed and sewed, until Chris returned.

When Chris returned, Mum and I were all ears to listen to his experience of America. He told us when he had arrived in New York how the Pastor had been horrified that he had gone all that way for just the one preaching engagement at his church. The Pastor had thought that Chris had others, so Chris hadn't dared confess to him that he only had a one-way ticket.

But Pastor Mercaldo took a liking to him, and loved his testimony and preaching manner, and treated him in first-class style. He decided to take Chris to a convention and introduced him to other pastors, who believed the well-respected New York Pastor's recommendation that they too would enjoy Chris's ministry. Not wanting to appear incompetent, Chris never mentioned to anyone about only having a one-way ticket. But he hadn't needed to. He was flown out especially to Indiana by Rev. Paul Paino to be his guest speaker. His massive church gave him a love gift which had been more than enough to get back to New York, and back home.

Chris told of the wonderful friendly American people, and the shock of discovering that they were absolutely nothing like the English had always believed them to be, and totally the opposite of the lady at the Embassy. How they were neither boasters, arrogant, or rude, and better mannered, and more humble, than even his own race. The best was his discovery of just how much they loved the English. His Mum and I listened for hours, as America and its people sounded like heaven.

--oOo--

It was time for us to leave Chris's Mum's house, to get to my Mom and Dad's house in The Straits Lower Gornal, to give birth at Rosemary Ednam Hospital, Dudley. My tapestry was nowhere near finished but I had lost interest now that Chris was back with me.

Wesley Adam, a lovely chunky bundle of 9 lbs 10oz

arrived on October twenty-eighth, 1970. I was absolutely thrilled we'd had another boy, and felt so proud to have two sons, and a brother for Calvin, who was just over the moon. His Dad rigged him out in a brand new set of clothes for his first visit to see his new brother in the hospital. On 4th January 1971, we had sailed away to be missionaries.

--oOo--

Now, November 1975, all five of us have been invited to go to America as a family. Now it is my turn to meet this friendly, seemingly misunderstood race. I can hardly take it in. Chris had mentioned the names of the unusual and exuberant people he had met. Now, I am going to meet them too.

I excitedly plan our get-away. Once in England, Chris will leave me and the children with my Mom and Dad, and go to America before me. We will follow two weeks later.

As we drive away from the Centro, I look back at it standing all alone in its vast ugly open space that gives me the creeps, and feel ashamed at how glad I am to be getting away from the sheer loneliness of it. I feel guilty at how I have come to loathe the Centro, with all its horrid beetles. We call at Lolita's shack and a few others to say goodbye. They all cry as if their hearts will break and as though they are never going to see us again. I feel sorry for them, the way they have come to depend on us, but not enough to stay. We ask Lolita's husband, if he would feed our animals for the time we are away.

When we arrive in England, Mom and Dad and Chris's Mum are thrilled about our trip to New York, but it isn't long before we find that not everyone is. It had been hard to swallow that Chris had already been invited to America at such a young age. Now the whole family were being flown over, all expenses paid. Such things didn't happen to people – let alone to missionaries.

Also, 'proper' missionaries are far too committed to leave their post to accept invitations to be flown half-way across the world. 'Proper' missionaries didn't look like me. 'Proper' missionaries should be plain, sombre, and too committed to being 'proper' missionaries to bother about something as vain as their image. 'Proper' missionaries stay out on their field, too busy living a life of sacrifice to go anywhere.

They are right. It is all true. We do not fit the image any more of what is portrayed as a proper missionary. We realize that our reputation as proper missionaries went long ago.

In England, a real missionary stays on the mission-field for years before even thinking of a home visit. The very sight of us again two and a half years after Cherry's birth isn't what commitment is all about. "Are you going to be coming back from the mission-field every twelve months from now then?" someone asks.

I tell Chris that because of all this, I won't be joining him in America after all, and to make apologies for me to his friends. I tell him I would rather not go than go through more pangs of rejection, or be the cause of further disappointment to people.

Chris thinks it hilarious, and can't believe it when he sees I am serious. "Miss an invitation to New York!?" he laughs. "Don't be so soft Christine. I thought you had well got over trying to please people, or wanting to live up to people's expectations. You ARE going to join me in America, and I am going to get the tickets right now, and that's final."

Chris returns with the tickets, ignoring all my objections. While he is away in New York, I go to the travel agent. I need to know what it is like going to America and what is expected. The agent tells me that New York is freezing cold in November, and to be sure to take warm clothing for the bitterly cold windy streets of New York.

Well warm clothing was something we didn't have any more, and there was no money to buy any. Mom and Dad weren't well off any more to help. But I knew someone who was. I would just have to swallow my pride and ask for her help. It will be embarrassing, but I can't arrive in New York in flimsy clothing, looking like a waif.

My sister Lily is the Matron of a hospital. She is a kind and helpful person, and I need to borrow some clothes. I am pleased when Lily is absolutely thrilled on hearing about my invitation to New York. She runs up to her bedroom excited, telling me to follow. She flings open a wardrobe overflowing with beautiful clothes asking me to choose what I want.

She gets into the swing of things, as if it is her who is going. She starts pulling garment after garment from her very expensive new stock of winter clothes, urging me to choose. But it is really Lily who will do the choosing.

"Christine!" she says in her high pitch matronly voice. "The very last thing you must NOT do is let the Americans think that the English don't know how to dress! So you MUST go appropriately dressed in my brand new winter wardrobe."

My kind sister tells you what to do, and you just find yourself doing it somehow, wondering why later. Everything she does must be done properly. Even a short, casual visit to her lovely big home means being shown to the 'formal sitting room' for tea in bone-china teacups, and red – never pink – dainty salmon sandwiches cut into the tiniest of triangles; crusts removed. A disposable cup or paper plate would never be found in her kitchen. A two-week holiday in even a well developed country, is as 'un-English' as she ever will get, and is a reminder not to make it three weeks next time.

I am relieved and grateful how she is being of help, and I do need the clothes. However, Lillian is taking a bit too much interest because she is convinced I could bump into a film-star in New York!

She pulls out a brand new coat, with a ridiculously high price tag still hanging on the sleeve. She tells me in no uncertain terms, in her shrill, overly-concerned voice, "Christine! You must travel in THIS coat, so that you will look presentable on arrival when your friends meet you at the airport. First impressions count you know and you need to look as 'posh' as an American. But it will also keep you warm in New York."

The thick heavy tweed coat has a deep, luxurious long haired, vivid ginger fox fur collar, and the fur plunges right down to the waist. The fur stands so high about the neck, I can only just about peep through. Fur has always made my nose tickle. It feels like I am drowning in it.

"Chris's friends will be so proud of you in this set Christine," she states, her arms suddenly overflowing with the big matching massive Busby-type fox fur hat, fox fur boots, and fox fur hand-bag.

Lily is much taller than me, so the coat is too long, and isn't me at all, so I try to make an excuse so as not to offend. "Lily, I'm going to be travelling for a total of fifteen hours, with three small children, the coat is in danger of getting spoiled on such a long journey."

But it doesn't work, and Lily replies, "Nonsense! Nonsense! And if it does, it doesn't matter. I'll just buy another one. Just don't forget to tell them Christine that you have a sister who would also like to come over to New York one day!"

We arrive in New York, after a long journey to London, then a plane ride of another seven hours with three small children and all our bags.

On arriving at the airport, I am in total shock on seeing that no one is dressed 'posh' at all. In fact, all I can see are ordinary people in very ordinary clothes. I am convinced that we can't have landed in America as it is nothing like the America I've seen on TV films. I am panicking that we could have boarded the wrong plane – something I was already worried about, as I struggled alone trying to make out if I had the correct long corridor. It had been nerve racking. It was all something new to me, airports, crowds, and so many ways to get lost.

I am convinced we could have boarded the wrong plane. The children stare at me wondering what is wrong. I am absolutely melting underneath Lily's thick tweed coat while peeping through fur, but can't take it off, as I have no way of carrying anything else.

Eventually, after all the palaver and waiting for cases, and lengthy checks at borders, I am so relieved as the doors slide open, to see Chris's smiling face with his friends. I can tell however, as my husband's eyes meet mine, and as his smile melts into a jaw drop, that he knows immediately that I have been to see my sister. I am so embarrassed for him and I look and feel an utter fool struggling into an unbelievable glamorous car as big as a tank, in seventy degree heat in a thick coat that is too long. Everyone is dressed so casual, even the Pastor and his wife who have picked us up. The image my sister and I had of America and Americans, had been one of glamorous clothes draped over glamorous people – like those who came to the Town Hall. But it was only me, the missionary, who looked like the rich film star, and an utterly foolish one at that.

Everyone sounds like a Charlton Heston or a John Wayne, yet seem so ordinary and unassuming, and totally unaware of the big over confident impression they make.

We cruise down an American highway, alongside unbelievably massive vehicles, which we'd only seen the likes of on an American film on T.V. The passengers in these cars look like puppets, and I cannot take it in that I am here in one. I can't understand what Pastor Mercaldo or his very attractive wife Evangeline are saying to me and I am completely thrown by the very different way they express things. I feel uneducated, inferior, and shy. I have to keep asking Chris to repeat what they have said to me, which makes me feel even more stupid. I am so ashamed of my awful West Midlands accent, which is making me want to keep my mouth well and truly shut.

I am overwhelmed by the Pastor and his wife. They are nothing less than sheer class and elegance. Even in casual clothes, they still resemble film stars, being so well groomed, posh and classy. The way they communicate with such respect and patience, without ever interrupting, is all such a culture shock.

We drive over bridges so high and long, it is breathtaking. There isn't a squeak from the children, who stare in disbelief as the Pastor points out magical words like the Statue of Liberty, the New York skyline, the Staten Island Ferry, the Rockefeller Center. It is like watching a movie that we are in.

Then above all things, the Pastor and his wife tell me what a lovely accent I have! I am even more speechless on hearing someone say that a West Midland accent is lovely.

It still doesn't make me want to say much.

We are taken to the Pastor's beautiful home on Staten Island, which is in the church grounds. Their home is marvellous and utter bliss. We are shown into their basement, which will be our own private living space.

Chris and I throw ourselves into each other's arms as soon as we are alone after not seeing each other for two weeks. Then he asks why I went to my sister's for clothes.

I am unable to take in what is happening to us, and why we are being treated like Royalty. We have a table-tennis table, a fridge crammed with delicious cakes covered in thick cream that my Mom would die for, and all kinds of treats for the children. The bathroom is colour-coordinated, with towels so lush and so soft, I will have to keep bathing. The water is soft like silk, the toilet rolls thick and patterned. We have a big colour television with constant cartoons. The children can't take their eyes off the screen, as they sit on deep lush carpet to watch it. The children unwittingly change channels, not knowing what is a remote, and we can hardly believe that someone is actually preaching on the television. We had never heard of such a thing. It feels like we have arrived to a country in Revival, especially after living with Civil Guards and machine guns.

This family care about us. I feel inadequate, and am too scared to speak, my vocabulary seems simple in comparison. Tim and Debbie, the Pastor's children, are so full of confidence, completely unaware of how overpowering they come over to our children, and I wish ours weren't so shy. Tim and Debbie are also unaware as to all the luxury they are living in, as America is just home to them, and they've known nothing else. There is no attitude of superiority, and their interest in such an ordinary English family is humbling. They are just bubbling with excitement to have us in their home, and keep asking if there is anything we need. Tim and Debbie even say they will take our children shopping. Our kids just stand speechless, as if they have arrived on another planet, and only relax when the family have gone upstairs.

It is a 'touch-button' country of convenience. The 'does it all' washing machine would fill my kitchen. The double door fridge with instant ice looks like a wardrobe. I am sure that Chris and I will lose each other in the humongous king sized bed. They even have a machine that washes the crockery for them, and a machine that cooks a potato in five minutes called a 'microwave'. It has been so long since I answered a telephone, and we have one at our disposal. There is an intercom connected to us downstairs for any need we have, and a sound system running through the entire house which plays beautiful soothing Christian music, and which we can control from the basement. The whole atmosphere is one of peace, love and joy. It is making me excited about heaven, which has to better than this, or it wouldn't be heaven to an American.

After arriving to the luxury of the basement, I just want to stay on our massive, deep cushioned sofa and enjoy all the goodies, but Chris says that we have to attend Church, and we have been given two hours to get ready.

When we arrive at church I am horrified! It is no ordinary service. We are the special guests, and I am dismayed to be making an entrance and to see everyone standing up, waiting to see Chris's wife and children. I am devastated and feel like the movie star my sister said I may meet. I can't believe why Chris hadn't said a word about it to me, knowing how I cannot cope with attention.

The people of the church have prepared a special celebration just for our visit. The theme is called 'Christmas in November'. All around the platform – which is a stage – there are piles of presents, all wrapped in sparkling paper and beautiful ribbons, with tags that say, Cherry, Wesley, Calvin, and Christine. There are long tables full of glorious food.

I don't like surprises or being surprised, but my worst ever surprise is yet to come. I am asked to be seated on the platform with Chris – the children too! All I want is to sit on a back row – but the pastor laughs when I ask if I can, as if I am joking. Then, to my horror, the Pastor tells us how we will all be speaking in turn! I know I am in trouble! I can't cope, and I try to get Chris's attention, but he is seated on the opposite side of the platform. I keep looking across hoping he will see the panic in my eyes. I really feel I am going to faint, going hot then cold. My heart is thumping so loud, I am sure the Pastor will hear it and let me get to that back row.

I am informed that these people are all waiting to hear from ME! They have already heard Chris, and these gentle, friendly, happy people have done so much for our visit, and are waiting to hear what I have to say. I am ashamed knowing how they are going to be disappointed, and how I will let Chris down.

With the journey to London, the seven hour flight, and the journey from JFK airport, plus all the time waiting at airports, we have been travelling for longer than twenty hours, and it is now two o' clock in the morning to us. The platform keeps rising to meet me as I struggle not to sway.

I keep glancing at Calvin, Wesley, and Cherry, who have been placed far from us, and can see how tired and confused and overwhelmed they are by masses of eyes fixed on them. If only Chris had warned me. He probably knows I wouldn't have come. He would have been dead right.

I know no one will be able to understand a word I say, because of the problems we had coming from the airport. What have I got to say to them anyway? I haven't a clue what these people would want to hear from me. The music and singing begins and everything is so overwhelmingly talented and professional. It is like being in the huge conventions at the Birmingham Town Hall – the only difference is – I am one of the speakers!!

As young people back in UK, we would do anything to get the best seats to be as close as we could to the American speaker on the Birmingham Town Hall stage. Now I am on a stage with an American Pastor, while an American congregation are waiting to hear me, Christine Smith speak, and I am terrified!

I cannot take in the high opinion everyone has of a missionary. The Pastor is leading the service and talks about us as if a King and Queen has arrived, saying we are special. I had never heard of human beings being called 'special' before. It isn't part of an English vocabulary.

I had overlooked asking Chris about my new image, but I am so relieved to see it had been unnecessary. Church is where they dress up. Every woman is wearing earrings. Every woman is wearing lipstick. Every woman is wearing flashy jewellery. Every woman has big lacquered hairstyles. Yet, they are the most God loving people I have ever seen. I would have looked odd and plain if I had arrived here with pale lips. I won't be seen as backslidden at all.

Whatever can I say to make them feel appreciated for the sacrifices of this 'Christmas in November?' How can I show how grateful we are?

Calvin, Wesley, and Cherry are the first to be stood in front of a huge microphone and it is lowered down to their height, intimidating them even more. I feel so sorry for them, and just want to scoop them up and say sorry to everyone that they are unable speak, seeing the fear on their faces. They have never seen a microphone, and stare at it, unable to let out one tiny squeak in answer to Pastor Mercaldo's questions, especially on seeing how a microphone will magnify anything they do say. I feel sorry for the Pastor who eventually has to give up on them, as they stand rooted to the spot like zombies, while cameras flash. The congregation express "aahhhss" to comfort the children. I can tell the children feel they have failed at something and long for me to go over to comfort them, yet I am so worried about doing something that could embarrass Chris. I don't know if it would be acceptable to walk right across a stage here, but I am rooted to the spot anyway. This is a bigger culture shock than when I arrived in Cuevas. I can't believe how the other half of the world lives.

Thought after thought flashes through my mind of what I can possibly say as my turn to speak gets nearer. No one has advised me of what they would want to hear. I already suffer with social phobia, which is nothing to the phobia I have of public speaking, and I know I will not get through it. All I can think to say is how lovely it is to be in a country where everyone is a Christian, and where there is Christian radio and television, but that's something they already know. I would love to say what a surprise it is to discover how lovely and friendly the Americans are, but that won't sound quite right either.

Yet it's true that everyone seems to be Christian. When we were picked up at the airport, we had stopped for a meal. The long menu was so baffling. There was food from every country in the world and we had never seen meals so huge. We thought at first that meals were brought on one communal plate for an entire table. The waiters and waitresses had joined in with the Pastor's grace and talked to him about church as if they were Christians, but they weren't. We couldn't believe the respect for Christians and ministers. Then the Pastor kept introducing us to anyone who entered the restaurant, as English missionaries. It was like a family, everyone so exuberant, respectful, and friendly. Living in a place where we are under the threat of Civil Guards day in and day out, such freedom felt overwhelming.

I am panicking. It is my turn to speak. The only feeling I have ever had similar to this, is when I am about to have an injection. I stand up, and much to my horror they clap. I have never ever heard people clap in a service before. The Pastor introduces me as Chris's 'help-meet' on the mission-field – at least he has that bit right. There is flash photography and because bright lights give me migraines, I know I am in deep trouble.

It's as if these people have made up their mind to love and like me before I have even spoken. There is just a sense of approval.

I begin. "It is so lovely to arrive in New York, where everybody is a Christian."

There is loud laughter as if I have cracked the funniest of jokes, and I hear a few remarks like, "She's a comedienne like her husband." Fortunately for me, the Pastor senses my stage fright and begins to ask me questions, which I then just need to answer. My agony is over and as I go to sit down the clapping continues.

It is time for Chris to preach. He is incredible, and I cry and laugh. Although I have heard him preach and teach as a Pastor, this is the first time I have heard him preach in his own language for a long time. His confidence still fascinates me, and I could listen to him all night. To me, his charismatic personality and humour is unique.

The congregation love him. His manner in speaking to these people has certainly made up for the children not speaking or any mistakes I made. He is also a natural entertainer. As I note his sense of humour, and his charisma as a speaker, I have to admire the grace he shows living in such a backward mission-field, when he could be doing this instead. He never as much as mentioned that he is a 'hole-digger', and I think it may be because he is embarrassed about being one.

The service is over. A party begins! It is time to open the huge amounts of 'Christmas in November' presents, starting with the children. At last, the children begin to relax a little, as they are urged to open one gift after another. There are toys, books, and the most exquisite of clothes. I open my presents of fabulous clothes, scripture gifts, books, tapes, magazines, make-up, jewellery, and perfume. I am so glad I wore make-up as they would have felt they had wasted their efforts. It mustn't have occurred to them that there are Christians in the world who think make-up is wrong. I can tell how these women think women should look their best in church.

At last, I have the opportunity to ask Chris why on earth he hadn't mentioned a word about this big 'do,' knowing what I am like. He said he'd had orders not to!

I had never realized, until this moment, that I had needed any appreciation. It feels as though I have been scooped up into the biggest pair of arms – every emotion hugged. I feel loved, accepted, even admired. I just want to stay here forever, and have to push the thought of going back to lonely Centro Cristiano from my mind. I am unable to take in that America is on the same planet as

England, let alone Spain. It feels like discovering a long, lost family. I feel like the prodigal must have done, when he came home to his Dad after living in a pig pen, being lonely and cut off from his family. I fit. I feel I may even be an American somewhere down the line. I know I was born to be as free as this.

All the pain of losing a denomination, and the loss of my reputation and culture, and family relationships, has vanished in one big swoop. We are being treated like Royals. Whenever we mention anything, no matter what, at the mere mention of it, we are doing it, having it, seeing it, eating it, buying it. So much so, I have to keep stopping myself from admiring anything, as when I admired one lady's coat, she took it off and gave it to me!

I can't believe how much I have found. I have found a new people, new friends, a new life, and the Lord knew it all along. How I wished I'd have trusted Him more.

It takes faith… to believe he has a plan.

I am so pleased Chris booked my ticket and ignored all my objections to coming, to be looked after, pampered, and taken places that dreams are made of. Chris has even been given the use of a huge Church vehicle with Calvary Temple written on it. The children look like ants sitting inside. I can't believe my husband is actually cruising around New York! It's like a dream. Although it is only November, people have Christmas lights in their gardens. The incredible displays are like Blackpool illuminations, and we have to keep stopping to take in each one. We have never seen Christmas displays in people's gardens ever.

I am amazed on seeing so many huge Churches, one after another and each more grand and beautiful than the next. And as for the shops, I am speechless. They are nothing less than warehouses. Whenever I see a huge red letter K I tell Chris to get to it as fast as he can. I want to keep walking around and around it, but my feet hurt so much after going through rail upon rail of clothes, at prices we wouldn't have dreamed possible. In England, people buy one garment. Here, people push trolleys tumbling over with clothes. I have bought umpteen garments at one dollar each. Then we see another warehouse shop, which isn't a religious shop, yet is still full of scriptural items. I want to take every one of them back to the Centro to plaster every wall. It seems so easy to be a Christian in America. No one has to hide it or keep it a secret. Then we go to what is called a 'Mall', which sounds somewhere where people 'mall around'. We discover that they are literally undercover 'cities'.

Complete strangers keep stopping to politely ask us where we are from, and then ask what church we will be speaking at.

Then of all things, we climb the Statue of Liberty. What a sight of New York through the crown for a nobody from the Midlands. Then we go up the Twin Towers, and the Empire State building.

But Pastor Mercaldo and his wife have the biggest surprise ever for us. They have arranged for people from the church to look after the children while they take us out for an evening. They take us to downtown New York. First, we have a grand meal with Pastor Mercaldo and his wife. Then we find ourselves in a New York Taxi. We are dropped off at the Radio City Music Hall of all places! I am speechless. I had never ever entered a cinema in my life. Although I had changed quite a lot, as yet, going to a cinema was something else. Now, it is my turn not to judge, because we are watching 'The Rockettes' live! The Pastor and his wife just want to give us a wonderful time.

The next day, at Calvary Temple, everything is spoiled. They have another surprise for me. I am to speak at a class! I am panic-stricken again. Everyone seems to be brought up to speak into microphones. Even if they are only two years of age they can do it so well, while I freeze at the very sight of one, and feel stupid because of it. But to my relief, I find it is a Sunday school class I am to speak in and I am comfortable with children. But when the time comes, they don't understand a word I am saying, or I them. So the Sunday school teacher, Lorraine, has to stand next to me to explain. With her arm affectionately around me, she starts to tell the children all about me.

Lorraine has a particularly strong twangy New York accent and her high pitched voice gets higher and higher as she explains things about me, "And do you know whaaaaaat children?" All the children gasp waiting for what. "Our missionary Christine who is here with us today doesn't have the things that we have here in America," and Lorraine gives me an admiring smile. "You see children, this missionary can't get the things on the mission-field that we are privileged to get here in America." So as well as the children, I too am waiting to see what this missionary doesn't have, and I am so hoping Lorraine hasn't found out we don't have proper toilets, or anything else that will make us look backward. Then Lorraine starts emphasizing louder and more pronounced what a sacrificial life I lead. "Do you know children, this missionary actually lives and works for Jesus, where you can't even get PIZZA!" The room fills with gasps, and jaws drop, which turn to admiring looks at the missionary who is living without Pizza.

I am completely in the dark as to what Pizza is, and don't know whether it is animal, vegetable, or mineral. I have only heard of the Tower of Pisa. But whatever this

PIZZA is that I am living without, it would be a terrible thing to have to do without for these polite and lovely children.

I have discovered the most important priority in an American child's life is Pizza, whatever it may be. Lorraine had successfully shown the children how they could identify with the life of a missionary, by saying it was like living without Pizza.

After the class is over, I ask Lorraine what Pizza is, but don't quite get an answer. A while later a van arrives with Pizza written on it. A man carries a massive square box with Pizza on it to the Sunday school door, which is then presented to *me*. A delicious smell is coming from the box, and I am amazed on opening it to discover that Pizza is an entire meal. Not only do they have ready made meals, but ones delivered right to a door. This country loves convenience.

This country is captivating. Its people bubble and ooze excitement, encouragement, motivation, and show such respect for each other. But above all, they are so loving and generous to the Lord's people.

Our farewell service is wonderful. When we had gone to the mission-field in faith we'd never had a proper 'send-off' or an official farewell. The farewell service is like being sent-out as missionaries for the very first time.

We also have something else we have never had up to now. We have a financial pledge every month from Calvary Temple. I wondered if it would still be living in faith having an actual pledge.

Our little family is driven to the airport in absolute style, clutching new bags, teddies, dolls, and wearing all new American clothes. We have brand new luggage stuffed full of towels, bedding, clothes, tapes, and scriptural items for Centro Cristiano. We even have Bibles on tape in the Spanish language for some of the people we reach who can't read.

There is an air of importance and spirituality to our departure as we are prayed over at the airport, which even the airport staff takes an interest in.

So God did have a plan after all!

It could take faith... to believe He has a plan.

I know in reality, that the God who spoke the universe into being, the Lord of Hosts who named each of His stars, the Creator of the sun and moon, the Almighty who is working out the Kingdom, has to have far bigger purposes and plans than sending little old me to America!

So my thoughts turn to God's purposes and plans and how they were established long ago.

"God causes all things to work together for good, to those who love God, to those who are called according (agreeing; harmony) to *His* purpose." (Romans 8:28)

This scripture was always used for anything that hadn't turned out like a person thought. It was that one comforting scripture that fit any human error or coincidence.

Now I see it in a different light. It is HE who has the purpose. It is HE who has the plans, and it is us who need to know what they are and graciously ask Him if we can have a part in accomplishing them with Him. Then we truly could be "those who are called" – and know without doubt that whatever happens, "God is causing all things to work together for good." .

Before, it seemed as if it was us – the created – who had all the plans and purposes, and invited God to come in on ours.

It could take faith... to believe He has the plan.

14

It Could Take Faith…
not to spoil the fun

Our ducks, chickens and rabbits are all dead! Lolita's husband has told us, that while we had been away, they had contracted some disease and had all died. Chris isn't convinced, and thinks it is more like a serious case of being eaten, knowing Lolita's husband. The children are upset and Centro Cristiano has never felt as lifeless.

I lie in bed, in the darkness of our wilderness, trying to keep alive my memories of America, re-living every single luxurious moment of it. It feels at times that I must have only dreamt about the freedom there, and being addressed as Ma'am, and the all-you-can-eat buffets. My favourite meal was a roast beef sandwich. We had longed for meat for so long and couldn't have got more than what was on a New York deli roast beef sandwich in an all-American Diner. The fresh sliced roast beef was piled so high, it would be a struggle for any size mouth to open wide enough to bite into it.

It was amazing to us how Americans were never

surprised about anything they had in their own country. Every time we were amazed, they were tickled at us being amazed. I lie in bed thinking about monster supermarkets which simply never closed, and how Chris and I would lose each other in them and then be told to get 'paged.' Shopping wasn't just shopping it was a day's outing. Now I am walking through a ragged curtain again pointing at a bucket of boring dried beans.

In all my experience of being in America, there had only been two things I had disliked. I could never understand why there would only be half a toilet door on a toilet facility in such a wealthy country. People could be touching up their make-up while someone had to use a toilet with half a saloon-type toilet door – and even that was slatted. I was paranoid about it, and the shop fitting rooms were the same. The other thing I disliked was the static shocks we kept getting from shopping trolleys and car door handles.

After returning from America, we desperately want to get into Cuevas, just to hear some life. My disappointment at not being able to get there has long worn off. I loathe the thought of living one moment longer in this solitude, even though the Centro is still proving to be a blessing. It is an ideal location for meetings for those afraid to attend our village meetings. Chris drives a long way to collect people to bring them to the Centro, then drives them all the way back home again. Some villagers hide while they wait for Chris. I call them secret disciples, like Nicodemus.

Chris and I have never ceased searching in Cuevas, hoping, and praying for a place since we arrived four years ago.

Apart from the meetings at the Centro, and outreaches in the caves of Cuevas, and in the open air, the longing to be right in the village of Cuevas continues. I daydream of being surrounded by neighbours, and to hear the sounds of everyday life, not to mention the children who would benefit to waking up to a street of children.

I feel so lonely, and never would have imagined that I would actually be longing to take our children to live in that squalor, just to hear something other than crickets. In addition, I am disheartened about the response to the Gospel, expecting to have seen more, especially how I pray and weep for souls for hours alone in our meeting hall whenever Chris goes out.

I am hoping that living in this wilderness isn't a lifetime call. We still don't have a telephone. I so enjoyed being connected in New York. There is still the one phone-office in Garrucha. Being here still means living in oblivion. Nothing could ever change. Progress could never happen here. It is a neglected poor unknown corner and it will always be that way. 'Mañana' is a fixed way of life here.

It isn't returning from America that has depressed me, quite the opposite. Going to America has helped. It is easy to see why it is such a blessed country. I'd never seen such love, respect, and appreciation for their pastors and anyone in the Lord's work.

Day after day as if I am watching the same film, I go over every single second of my pampered two week visit, knowing just how privileged I was, and wondering if I will ever experience such heaven again. It has given me hope. I have the knowledge that we have a new church that cares about us and prays for us.

I have also gained a whole new enjoyment and satisfaction from being a missionary at all. It is because of being a missionary that I had been invited to go to America in the first place. Going to America, had actually increased my excitement of heaven. "Just imagine," I often say to

Chris, "If we hadn't obeyed the Lord in coming to Spain, I'd never have gone to America and sampled such bliss." Chris always answers with, "Yes, and you wouldn't have gone if I hadn't have insisted on booking your ticket!"

It was little old me, in 1975, a nobody from Dudley, who had been up the Twin Towers, the Empire State building, the Statue Of Liberty, and to Radio City. Nevertheless, it was the people that made America exciting.

Amongst all the worship tapes I had been given, there was one in particular, proving to be such a great comfort on returning to a lifeless wilderness. I play it so often I'm concerned the words will wear off. She sings, "He's got all the time in the world," and "He knows what temptation can do, DON'T GIVE UP..."

After mixing with so many Christians in New York, Chris and I crave a chat with some Christian friends or family about everything. We know we should have shared our heartache about Cuevas with our new American friends, but whatever concern was on my heart, it had certainly been wiped out of my mind within seconds of arriving to such a welcome.

We would love to talk to someone about the whole experience, and the wonderful new friends we had made in America and the incredible time we'd had, and how the Lord had blessed us. I am wondering if there is a time limit on a prayer. We have been praying about Cuevas for a long time, but just as I feel like giving up, she sings again, "Don't give up."

I feel a disappointment to the Lord, as I can't pretend not to want to be surrounded by people. He knows everything. I can't pretend I am happy. At least I have almost succeeded in living bug-free. Every morning I mop the floors, and apply a fresh line of bug-powder around all the edges of windows and doors, and even puff the powder inside cupboards and behind everything. Bug-powder is my favourite substance here. I will find which hole any monster comes from, mix plaster and fill it myself. Hardly any bug wants to step over our threshold now.

One day, Chris arrives home from the post office excited. "Christine, look what I have," he says, waving a letter. "It's from my brother and his wife. They are planning to take a holiday in Benidorm with a little group from their church. Let's plan to drive up there to be with them." I immediately start packing and making my famous 'to do' lists – how Chris hates my 'to do' lists. Even though the trip is six months off, it has brought some instant relief.

The group are going to Benidorm, a new tourist area which Franco has permitted to be, all supposedly to do with bringing in money, but we think it is more a cover up for how the rest of his country lives in dire poverty.

The days, weeks, and months drag by. My excitement heightens as the time draws near for me to be able to share my hurts, heartaches, and loneliness, and above all our unique American experience with someone at last. I am also pleased that Calvin and Wesley will be able to get together with their cousins: little dark haired beauty Cheryl, and Mark.

After a steaming hot five hour drive on narrow roads around mountains, we eventually arrive in Benidorm, and it is a shock. Why couldn't we have been called here? We can't believe the absence of goats, flies, donkeys and carts. It is a small patch of paradise in Spain. It is English tour operators who have discovered sea, sand, and cheap wine in Benidorm. They have created a holiday-haven get-away especially for the sun-deprived English, all donkeys and carts removed.

We are excited as we search for a place to stay before we find Chris's family. We go from one hotel to another to find the cheapest, but are puzzled why every room is priced the same, even if overlooking the beach. So obviously we choose a room overlooking the tranquil Mediterranean. The noise, laughing, and fun going on underneath our little balcony, stirs up an even stronger desire to live with sounds, even if does have to be in Cuevas.

The water in our room still isn't fit to drink and still goes off for hours, as does the electricity. The shower splutters out scalding or cold water. The toilet doesn't flush properly, there's a smell of sewage, and the plumbing is so inadequate that the water doesn't go down the sink. However, nothing seems to be doing anything to deter the English from coming to Benidorm. Being starved of sunshine gives them a tolerance factor for two reliable weeks of sunshine, as they would never put up with such facilities back home in England.

A bit of the Spain we are more used to comes about. As Chris is walking down the street, he is grabbed by a Civil Guard, and poked in the chest. Chris is abruptly told to put his shirt on, and that he can only be without a shirt if on the beach.

It is obvious as we watch the English, that the two coves in Benidorm possess an ability to tranquilize and soothe away troubles in one glorious sun-soaked, sun-bathing day. We know the English. Their aim throughout the year will be to work and save every penny to have an annual Benidorm holiday, no matter how cold or hot the shower, where the sun is as reliable as the rain back home.

We locate the group. I only have one thing on my mind – to pour out my unhappiness and loneliness about Cuevas, and to share with someone about our New York experience. I have waited six long months for this. I can hardly wait to unload and to have my emotions hugged again like in America. We are with family, and I just need to cry on a shoulder. To us, the holiday isn't too important. We have only just had one in America. It is the people we have come to be with.

The English are usually docile, but this place must have strange powers. We can't be watching our own race. They don't normally let go, or laugh at themselves. It seems their deep disgust for ruined picnics, wet bank holidays, and rainy weekends in England, dampens what they may really be capable of.

Although they are a free race, it seems they must only discover that fact after leaving the shores of England. It is the first time we have seen the English lose their inhibitions.

The group is situated in a hotel that is located in the back part of Benidorm, squashed between two old properties and quite a walk from the sea. We learn that our beautiful room overlooking the sea, has cost nothing – being an out of season on-the-spot booking – in comparison to what they had paid for their pre-booked package. However, the English are good at making the best of anything.

They are basking and revelling in this up-and-coming exciting new paradise haven, and no shabby hotel will stop that. We had never seen the English so free. The serious have become jovial, the burdened free, the quiet verbal, and the prude even a bit rude! They are not going to be back on the neat wet streets of England for two whole weeks, and will be lapping up fourteen glorious days of absence from worries and cares, replaced by sun, sea, and imported sand.

I watch them all having fun in the pool, and Calvin and his cousins playing together. Our families are together for a little while. My heart is almost breaking at the thought of returning to emptiness and loneliness for another four years. I pretend to be happy, just waiting for the right time to tell them how miserable I really am, and also to chat about our new American friends in New York, and our unbelievable time there.

Everyone is drinking in the atmosphere. The group even have a special meeting together, to excitedly discuss what they are going to do the next day, whether to shop, walk, sight see, or swim, and how not a minute on indecision must be wasted.

I keep waiting for the proper time to share my burden. But as the first week goes into the second, the opportunity seems to be slipping away. Now I am hoping they will delve, to ask how things are to trigger it off. But no one does. I almost feel invisible. I don't feel free to share or ask for help any more. It could dampen everyone's spirit and spoil everybody's fun. It suddenly seems inappropriate to blurt out my cares. It could come over as selfish or complaining, and could seem as if the only reason for our sickly day's drive had been a selfish one.

Another thought comes to mind. How everyone is probably escaping from their own troubles and pressures of life for two weeks before having to face them again, so why should they have to listen to mine? If every time I appear on the beach, and they have to listen to me moan, they will lose hours of their precious holiday.

As well as seeming inappropriate to unload, it also seems inappropriate somehow to tell everyone about our exciting trip to America and our star treatment there. What if they see it as boasting? I think too, that I may also be confused about our trip to America, where we were pampered and made to feel important, and that it would be the same when we arrived in Benidorm. But we are just family. While they are on their annual holiday, how can I talk about somewhere we have been, that was so fabulous, that it will make their Benidorm holiday seem nothing in comparison? Also, it is us who have a room with a balcony overlooking the sea. We too are the ones wearing new American clothes, jewellery, and make-up, compared to their jaded summer clothes. Maybe it is us, in their opinion, fortunate enough to be able to have a room with a sea view, and to wake up every day to this glorious sunshine, while they have to be grateful for two short weeks in it. No one is going to believe we have a burden – because they haven't seen the real Spain.

It is almost time for everyone to leave, and every second is being grabbed to tilt heads back and hold faces up to the last bit of sun, knowing they won't see much of it until their next annual holiday. The appropriate time to cry on a shoulder never came. How I wish it was us going back to rain rather than to the Centro in the sun.

Just as the group are ready to leave, there is a terrible freakish storm, and the whole of Benidorm closes down as frightened people peep through doors and windows at rare torrential rain gushing down each street, and pink and purple lightning flashing across a black eerie sky, accompanied by deafening thunder. As we wave everyone off, I think I still would have liked for them to have enquired how life was for us here.

We start for home. As we pass through all the tiny villages a deathly silence is overwhelming in each. Everything is lifeless and people are sitting on door steps looking distressed and expressionless. Even children are walking instead of playing. Something bad has happened that we are unaware of.

The closer we get to home, the thicker an atmosphere of sadness. Then suddenly, without warning, the road on which we are driving isn't there. We get out of the car to discover absolute devastation. The road has caved in, and the stench is dreadful. There are trees, dead animals, upturned vehicles, and debris strewn everywhere. The whole place is an obvious flash flood disaster.

We have to turn around to try and find another way home. We stop to chat to villagers, each one heartbroken. We learn that the weird storm in Benidorm had become flash floods further south, and it had happened on a Saturday when peasants use dry riverbeds to transport home grown produce. The torrent of water from the mountains had swept away everything and everybody in its path.

I feel ashamed about my few problems, after seeing what people had gone through.

The sun isn't shining, showing just how morbid, drab and depressing these tiny, isolated villages would be without sunshine. There is a presence of death, and many lives have been lost.

During the last few miles of our journey, while needing to manoeuvre around rubble over and again, we suddenly realize that the Centro can't have escaped the flash flood either. It is bound to have been washed away too. It is inevitable. It is built close to the riverbed which goes through all these villages. Even the Doctor's wife had told us we shouldn't be living there. So she was right!

It was because of these very reasons, that people had poked fun at us for buying that particular piece of land and building on it. Chris says, "Christine, mistakes like this really matter when you are being watched and are the first to bring the Gospel to a place. How will we explain and face everyone?"

Now, we don't only have the embarrassment of not being able to get into Cuevas, but also the shame of a mission station and home we shed tears to build, that has been washed away. No mission station. No discernment.

Don Pedro and Concepción had given us the most problems for living where we had chosen to live, because of their concern for the children, mentioning the riverbed almost every time we went to see them. So much so, we had felt constrained to tell them private spiritual things, to ease their concern. We had explained that we felt guided by God to buy land and build there. They had started to believe us, mentioning the location of the Centro less and less, even wanting to know more about the scriptures. It will really matter to be able to explain this disaster so that we don't look foolish to any potential converts, spoiling trust. A reputation has become much more important to those outside the Church now.

Although I hadn't been content living at the Centro, I now admit that it is a better provision than the tent or caravan. Surely, it had to mean something that at the time of the flood, we all happened to be in Benidorm, somewhere it had taken six months to plan for, when we never usually went anywhere. Surely, it could be seen as a miracle that we hadn't been in the Centro at the time of the flash flood. What a testimony it could be for this awful mess! Now we have thought of a reason, I am fighting off twinges of gladness that it is washed away.

"Chris, where will we sleep tonight," I ask, "as the caravan will have been washed away too. What will we do? Where will we go? No one we know can accommodate us all. The Doctor is the only person who has a little more room than most, but it will be so embarrassing."

The next little bend will reveal the extent of the damage

to our little marvel. I bury my head in my hands and peep through my fingers. How I have hated the location of the Centro. How I have hated living in a barren isolated wilderness. Now I feel to blame.

But it can't be true! As we turn the bend, the Centro is still standing all in one piece, and sparkles in one brief outburst of sunshine, as if welcoming us back. Everything around it is in turmoil, and we dread going inside. We can hardly get to the door for rubble, the stench is incredible. Yet although the cascade of water had gushed right alongside the Centro, knocking down the surrounding walls, it hadn't entered the building.

It is more scary and eerie than ever, sleeping in a wilderness with the smell of dead animals, mud, and debris all around us. It will take forever to clean up. I now admit that I am never going to get away from the Centro. I have to accept it and will not try any more to get out of any inconveniences God's call involves. I decide that I won't pray any longer about getting into Cuevas. I will accept that at least Cuevas is still being evangelized for the first time ever – and even if we don't live there, it is a place we wouldn't have known existed but for the dream.

I am glad now that in Benidorm there hadn't been an appropriate time to cry on a shoulder. If this is God's call, I shouldn't want to. God shouldn't be made to look like a task master, by someone obeying a call just to grumble about it.

I thank the Lord for keeping our home safe. I thank the Lord that He didn't allow me to dampen anybody's fun in Benidorm. I thank the Lord he helped me resist the temptation to make anyone pity me. I thank the Lord for the unbelievable times in New York that I was able to keep in my heart, and for all the other things that our friends and relatives in Benidorm could only have dreamed of. I believe incredible times will come again.

I ask the Lord to help me never to spoil anybody's fun even if I may not be having any at the time. I ask the Lord to help me rejoice with people, and to be happy for them and around them.

I am aware however, that it may be a different story next time. It may get harder not to spoil someone's fun. What if the 'being blessed' is in the form of a family member being left in an uncle's will and we're not?

It could take faith... not to spoil the fun.

What if the 'being blessed' is their diet working perfectly, while mine fails? What if the 'being blessed' is their church or ministry thriving while ours is stagnant? What if the 'being blessed' is a friend having a nice new car, while our old one keeps breaking down?

What if the 'being blessed' is others enjoying a fabulous time on holiday while my heart is breaking.

It could take faith... not to spoil the fun.

"REJOICE *with* those who rejoice." (Romans 12:15)

The hardest word in that scripture isn't the word 'rejoice'. It is the word – *with*. It isn't enough to rejoice – inside – in silence. I have to rejoice *with*. My 'rejoice' has to be *seen*. I have to *show* it.

It could take faith... not to spoil the fun.

15

—

It Could Take Faith…

to enjoy

The village in the area that has suffered the most flood damage is Cuevas.

For the first time on arriving in Cuevas, we are not the focus. I had thought it impossible for Cuevas to be more squalid. The place is a disaster. People are in shock having lost family and friends.

Rain is so rare, that peasants use dry riverbeds to sell home produce, and the flash flood had happened on such a day.

We lean over remaining bits of a bridge, to see a ravine of mud, piled with vehicles, furniture, trees, swollen dead pigs, chickens, and goats. The flash flood was a torrent sweeping away everything in its path from miles away.

The worst affected part is the lower part of Cuevas – 'the ditch' I call it – because it is alongside the riverbed. The tiny terraces weren't up to much, but were people's homes.

As we step around mattresses, chairs, and clothes drying out on the street, we pass by a distressed man muttering.

He points out to us a tiny ground level building and says, "No one will ever risk living there now. People who lived in this lowest part have fled to the top of the village, and will never risk returning here. My little place is filled with mud; water reached to within inches of the ceiling."

The man is devastated, and says how hard he had worked to renovate a place he had planned to rent out. "People here just don't forget tragedies like this," he says. "The women will talk about it on these streets for years to come."

"So it's your place then?" Chris asks, both of us trying to resist showing too much enthusiasm on hearing that there's a place no one would risk living in.

"Yes, it's mine. I have built it. My name is Pablo. A friend of mine had been sleeping on the floor in it while I was finishing it off. I have to be thankful he managed to escape with his life just in the nick of time. The place will take forever to clean and dry out, but it will all be a waste of time, as no one would contemplate sleeping in a ground level dwelling, next to the riverbed." But his words are like a red rag to a bull to me. I would, I thought. Just give me the chance!

Chris casually asks the question we both know is burning inside both of us, on hearing at last that there is someone who will rent a place. "Pablo, is this place available to rent then?"

Pablo looks startled. "Well, yes, but what would you want it for?" he asks puzzled, looking at our children.

Chris says, "Well, we are the missionaries and we would like somewhere in Cuevas to rent as a meeting hall."

Pablo quickly changes, "No. No. I am very sorry. I can't rent it to you."

Our hearts sink, having felt that something had come up at last. We know we are facing the same old hostility.

Here is a person that has just told us how no one will live in the house, yet is refusing a chance to rent it. It will always be the same old predicament. Renting would mean an ongoing connection with the new preacher. But then Pablo says he has an idea. He says that although he can't rent it to us, he will sell it to us instead! Now it is our turn to say, "No. No. Sorry. Impossible." We explain how we only want a place to rent, but thank him for the offer.

But Pablo insists we listen. He goes on to say to pay him as if paying rent like we want, but that he and Chris will go together and register each instalment as a payment of sale. Then Pablo says when the instalments add up to the purchase price, he will give us a deed of sale. It sounds too good to be true, or like a desperate man.

Chris thinks Pablo has to be up to something, and he could be right, especially after what had happened with the Centro. One night, I had woken up at three o'clock in the morning with a frightful thought that we didn't own the land we had bought from Francisco! It was such a shock. We had been living at the Centro for two years. I woke Chris to tell him what I had felt, but he said it couldn't mean anything as the three of us had gone to sign and record payment for the land with a proper Notaria and had papers and a receipt. I tried hard to forget it, but I couldn't be put off. I knew it meant something. It made Chris uneasy. He explained it could be unwise to question, saying it wouldn't look good if we distrusted people, when things are already hard going here. Yet I knew we must speak to Francisco about it. Francisco just laughed, and said we would all go and register it in our names one of the days! At that, we insisted we all go to the Notaria together immediately. To our amazement, we found that although payment for the land had been recorded, it didn't mean that the land was ours! It had to be registered in our name, and at a particular land registry office. It took lots more paperwork for it to be legally ours.

So I can understand Chris's uncertainty about Pablo. I wish I could stop myself believing Pablo will keep his word. It is the only chance we will ever have to get into Cuevas.

Chris thinks me mad when he realizes, as well as having it for meetings, I am planning to live in the flood house.

But Chris doesn't feel as lonely as me and the children. "Christine, you can't be serious. It isn't big enough for a family to live in. It's a mere box. Are you forgetting just how close it is to the riverbed, and why the man could be making such an offer?" I tell him, that yes, I did realize all that.

Chris takes me to Cuevas. He shows me a door right next to the little house, which men keep going in and out of. It is a toilet. The toilet door doesn't close properly and the view is an embarrassing one and the smell worse. It is not only joined to Pablo's house, but is so near to the front lounge window of the little house, that the trail of men would be seen all day.

When Chris knows I had already seen it, and that it hadn't bothered me, he sees how desperate I must be. I know without doubt that I should be in that house.

I had always held a scriptural concept close to my heart, that the man should be the ultimate decision maker in the home. I had no intention of getting married with plans to manipulate, control or change a spouse. I wanted someone to be who they were, their own person. I had seen someone change their husband so much; he ended up a replica of his wife, and had lost his individuality and was boring company after that. But since living here, where one person owns all the brains in Spain, I don't only view control of another as just wrong or selfish any more. I now even see it – as stealing. It is being a thief to rob someone of their own desires, their own choices, their own personality. To want to own another's brain in addition to one's own – is greed, or covetousness. "Greed amounts to idolatry" (Colossians 3:5).

When I don't cease being excited about Pablo's offer, Chris is taken aback. Chris knows my excitement isn't a mischievous way of trying to get round him to get what I want. He knows how it affects me whenever I have seen my gender behave deviously. He also knows I don't sulk if I don't get my own way. So he is impressed that how I feel may mean something. It's as if he really does want the little house, but needed double assurance – and in this instance – I am it.

I tell him how convinced I am that the Lord will supply the 'rent', something very much on Chris's mind, knowing we will lose every payment if we falter even on one, as Pablo had made that clear. The house is £400 more than the £600 my Dad had sent us to the mission-field with. I also assure Chris how I am fully aware that there is never any indication of when a flash flood can happen, and how we had discovered this area has a tendency towards it. I tell him I am totally aware how near to the riverbed we will be sleeping, even closer than the mission-house is.

I also tell him, it could take faith… to enjoy.

When Chris is fully convinced that I know exactly what is involved, he goes back to see Pablo to see if he really meant what he said, or if it was just something to fob us off. Chris warns me how people change their mind here, and that Pablo could even have made other arrangements by now.

I wait at the Centro for his return. But I am unable to stop myself getting things together for a move. Four years of living at the Centro, and I know we're out. Calvin, Wesley, and Cherry will be able to mix with other children instead of getting out of bed to emptiness and no one.

Chris returns and says Pablo is sticking by his suggestion, but says we can't use the place for quite sometime as it will take so long to clean out the mud, and replace wiring. I am so disappointed.

But we eventually arrive at Cuevas and Pablo has done us proud. The miniature bungalow is clean, all walls whitewashed inside and out. It has new switches, new plugs, and there isn't a hint it has been full of mud.

Chris and I will have the back bedroom next to the kitchen. The lounge will be the very first meeting hall in Cuevas. Calvin and Wesley will have the windowless room off the lounge, and Cherry is in the brush cupboard!

People gather, muttering about us, and we realize the first problem of living right in a village. We are more on show, and our family will have to be careful and considerate to fit in. We are the first foreigners here, and the first missionaries. Certain aspects of our lives were hidden in the wilderness, and we had got used to doing what we wanted, how we wanted and when. Here we are right in the culture, and we will have to be careful not to offend. I intend to keep on the right side of these women at whatever cost.

But there is immediate hostility. They tell us it is thoughtless to allow children to sleep at ground level of a 'flood-house'. But I am so happy, that even their disapproval can't dent it, yet I stifle my joy so it doesn't look as though I don't care about their concern. I try to convince them not to worry as another flood won't happen for a long time, which makes things worse, as it is seen as flippancy.

I would really like to tell them that it is God's provision, but it will sound condescending, after the devastation they have gone through.

Noise is what I desired. Noise is what God has sent. Cuevas thrives on noise. No one speaks in a normal voice, everyone has to shout or scream to one another. Moms screech all day long, "MANOLO. NO. NO!" "ANTONIO. VEN AQUI!" (Come here!)

"PACO NO HAGAS ESO!" (Don't do that!). I know if I had arrived in Cuevas from the start I would have wanted to leave to save my eardrums.

Pablo had said that no one would ever return to their homes in the 'ditch.' But he was wrong. Within a year people are starting to clean out their houses. They gradually start to move back in. Our house though, is the only one on ground level.

Surprisingly, in Cuevas, the shops come to us. A bread van honks, the water lorry pips, a fish cart bellows, the milk cart hoots, and the knife sharpener just starts pedalling, and people appear with knives, scissors, and scythes. It seems everybody owns a pig or a rooster, and the roosters 'cock-a-doodle-doo' at five o'clock every morning. But I am where living souls are, and never want to live in silence again. The years of isolation are gone, even if the air isn't as fresh.

Even though our heads throb with all the noise, nothing can dampen my delight. But Chris can't wait to get off to the Centro for a while, to print tracts, study, and pray, glad to get away for a bit of peace and quiet, and some sweeter air. Now, I not only have a child at school, like a normal Mom, I also have a husband who goes out of the home to work.

My very favourite sound is the dropping of fresh water from our roof container into the taps. The water man fills the container every week, and it can be used for every function. Washing at the well in Mojacar is well and truly over. Pablo has even put a small 'pila' (stone washboard) on the tiny back patio for me. This is *that real 'escape route' from the Lord.* It is also the end of digging holes for Chris, because the rubbish is collected every day to keep down disease.

However, it is a shock on learning that Calvin isn't allowed back to the Vera school. They say it is not permitted now we live in Cuevas. The Cuevas School is far more backward than Vera. But Calvin is now a fully experienced little soldier, and although he is disappointed leaving his friends, we know he will get on with it and make new ones. He is once again the very first foreigner in another school, and will break the ice at this one too, making it easier for Wesley who will have to start school soon, and then Cherry.

The powers and authorities that be, are more intense in Cuevas. The whole village comes to a reverent halt more than once a day. Music, gongs, and bells precede rituals bombarded over the airwaves, as a reminder to be loyal to the system.

Watching the only little golden heads of Wesley, Calvin, and Cherry bobbing up and down as they run around the streets and play on the scruffy little children's park, which is right behind our bedroom window, is something I had dreamed of for them when listening to my song, "Don't give up." Calvin beams all the time, and loves playing marbles with Miguel, the son of the neighbours of the bar joined to our house. The bar makes something called 'tapas' which are bits of 'buena comida' and Calvin is quickly developing a taste for them. Calvin is becoming a true local.

Calvin comes rushing home one day and says how Miguel's Mom has given him something quite different and delicious to eat. Calvin isn't quite sure what 'gorrión' is, but says it was tasty. Chris and I weren't too impressed when we looked it up and found he had eaten a sparrow! Especially when the Bible says, "He sees the sparrow fall," and it was Calvin's throat He had seen it fall down! But Calvin isn't a bit perturbed, and just wants to fit in and try all things new. It made me think about something in the Bible. How five sparrows were sold for two farthings. I had never thought it may have been for sustenance.

Wesley is village entertainment and his antics crack any serious face. No one can resist laughing at his pranks because they love a mischievous little boy, and Wesley drops into this category. The villagers have named Cherry 'La Coqueta' (little show off). This is because she wears the most gorgeous organza dresses with frilly petticoats, matching frilly pantaloons, and socks. My sister Lily sends them over. They are the very expensive cast-offs of her two daughters, but the outfits look as if they have never been worn. Cherry sits most of the day on top of a big orange gas container looking like a little princess, watching people go by, and eating a 'bocadillo' – on it. She brightens up the ditch with her blonde pigtails, ribbons, and fancy frocks. Everyone stops to say, "Hola Coqueta."

Cherry is always the first to spot the water man for me, so we don't miss our vital quota of water. She shouts, "water-man mommy."

Wesley has a great weakness in the village. He goes limp with pity at all the starving dogs, and gets distraught at seeing their ribs poking out. Wes has a compassion for anything and everything that has four legs – or more. When we lived in the wilderness, he even pitied beetles! He collected them. When I looked into his little wheelbarrow one day to see what he was gathering, I almost threw up at the sight of the umpteen beetles he said he was taking for a ride.

Now, he is collecting wild dogs. We just cannot convince Wesley of the danger of stray dogs and the high risk of rabies if bitten. He just cannot help himself, and strolls home most days with several starving dogs trailing behind him. It's as if all the strays in Cuevas had been waiting for a friend like Wes to turn up, and that he is the answer to their miserable existence. All our leftovers keep on disappearing.

But we are afraid for Wes, knowing the risks from ticks, fleas, and above all, rabies. We decide to take Wesley to see our doctor friend. Wesley loves the doctor, and out of all three, the doctor is enamoured with Wes, merely because he's full of mischief. The doctor calls him "WE," as the Almerían miss off the 's' on their words. We want the doctor to explain to Wes how serious it is to go near wild dogs. The doctor is very concerned. He begins to tell 'WE' how he has seen people die in agony with rabies. Don Pedro then shows Wesley some huge injection needles. He then asks Wesley to pull up his top, and demonstrates. Don Pedro is so good at these 'demonstrations!' "Now WE," he says, "If one of those dogs bites you, you will need fifteen of these big injections right here in your tummy. And WE, the injections have to go into you one after the other. Fifteen, all in one go! And WE – that is very, very painful." Wes looks horrified and says he understands. But within days Wes is coming home with starving dogs behind him. There is no cure for Wes's compassion for his homeless four legged friends, even with a daily reminder of fifteen painful injections.

We have discovered where the off-key brass band practises all year round for the fiesta – right behind our bedroom window, on the children's park. I have learned that it is best to pay full attention to exactly what one desires from the Lord – as noise is what I had desired. The band practice can last until three in the morning, just before the 'cock-a-doodle-doos' start. We may give fiestas a miss from now on, after hearing distorted trumpets and clanging triangles for months on end.

Hearing annoying gongs and cymbals night after night, has made me think about 1 Corinthians 13. "If I speak with the tongues of men and of angels, but do not have love, I have become a noisy gong or a clanging cymbal…" It's hard to think of God having to hear such a row!

--oOo--

It is getting near Christmas, so Chris and I are having the usual discussion on what we will give the children, and also what to eat for Christmas dinner. It has to be a cured slimy salted ham, which I do not like, or choosing a live chicken. We may need to travel to 'El Corte Ingles' for a prepared chicken.

Chris comes back from the Post Office box one day with a note that we have a parcel at Zurgena. Zurgena is around a one hour journey, and is the railway station where we pick up any parcel for us. The journey always seems like two hours because of the excitement of what could be in the parcel. We always hope it will be something nice from home. I am anticipating that this parcel will be something that I will be able to wrap up as Christmas presents for the children. Our parcels are normally clothes for the poor which we take around the caves, or are the dresses for Cherry from my sister.

One time in a sweltering August, we received fifty hand knitted thick woollen hats. We were convinced that the missionary parcels had got mixed up and that the hats were expected in the North Pole.

Another time we received a box full of currants and raisins. They had taken so long to arrive it was a box of worms.

Then in one parcel, there were some beautiful brand new ladies clothes, with the price tags still on. There was one particularly gorgeous blue taffeta blouse with trumpet sleeves, and some elegant beige slacks. We distributed the clothing, and took some to Lolita's house. When we returned to her house for a meeting one evening, we were amazed to see her husband was going to stay for our meeting, something he had never done. He and most men saw it as weak and an interest for women. We would see it as a breakthrough if he came to our meeting. So we were ecstatic to see Lolita's husband – until our eyes had adjusted to the darkness inside the house that is.

Lolita's husband is not only a macho man, but has to constantly prove he is. He marches right out of the house when his wife begins to cook, sweep up, or change a baby. When Lolita's husband unexpectedly saw Chris helping me, he gave Chris a warning. He told Chris that no man would ever respect or listen to anything he had to say if they knew he did women's work.

Lolita told us how most of the men have mistresses, being part of having to be seen as real men, and that the wives have to accept it. She explained it to me one night, when I asked her why her husband wasn't home. She was genuinely surprised I didn't know the reason. She said, "Well, that's what real men are like Christine." She went on to explain, that as long as a husband doesn't abandon his wife, he not only calls himself a faithful husband, but truly believes he is one. Then Lolita had asked me, "Doesn't Chris then?" When I told her it would end our marriage, she answered, "Well, you see, it is the fiery blood the men have in them here Cristina," as if Chris didn't have any, so couldn't be a real man, but I could tell she was hurt by her husband's behaviour.

The Gypsy men – like the women – love wearing bright gaudy clothes. So Lolita's husband had stayed to the meeting just to show off some new flamboyant clothes he was wearing. Chris and I almost choked on seeing what clothes they were. He had on the bright blue shiny lady's silk blouse and lady's beige slacks, and was completely unaware that the clothes were women's attire. He sat so proudly grinning.

If Lolita's husband knew, he would never have let us into his house ever again, and would have also punished Lolita for not watching out for him properly. He hadn't a clue about the mistake he had made, but I could see that Lolita knew. It was her little bit of mischievous revenge on a lazy, unfaithful husband, as she had kept grinning and winking at me throughout the service.

We arrive in Zurgena in the hope that our parcel will have something that can be wrapped up for the children for Christmas morning. I am not disappointed when I take a secret peep into the box. My mother-in-law had informed me that she would be sending a parcel at some time. She had sent an entire box full of chocolate bars and sweets. I bless Mum and explain to the children that we can't open the parcel this time. But it gets impossible to keep the contents a secret. I am pestered until I eventually succumb, and all of us finish the whole lot off before we get home, and we all feel sick. I know Mum would be cross, as she had given strict instructions not to open any parcel that came until Christmas morning. Now there will be nothing on Christmas Day.

The next day, Chris comes from Garrucha waving a letter and a cheque, and can hardly get the news out quick enough. "Christine. Just look at this! A Church I preached at in America has sent us a Christmas gift." When I look at the cheque and read the letter, Chris is shocked at my lack of enthusiasm. "What's wrong love?" he asks. "Aren't you pleased?"

"Chris, this letter says that we are not to use any of this money for any other needs, other than our own, as it was the only reason it was given!"

Chris says, "So? What's wrong with that sweetie?" I can't imagine what we would spend such a huge amount on – but a whole range of reasons flood my mind why we shouldn't even try, and I don't know which to tell him first.

When we moved from the Centro to Cuevas, we didn't bring anything substantial with us. We had left everything the same at the Centro for the Lord's work at the mission house. So here in Cuevas, I feel more like a missionary. I am living how I perceived missionaries should live.

I had tried to settle the fact from the start, when becoming a missionary, that possessions and home comforts would be a thing of the past, something for others, not missionaries. The lack had actually brought me some pleasure and fulfilment at being a missionary.

I had been brought up watching my parents give and give to missionaries and ministers. Whatever evangelist, minister, or missionary came Dad's way, Dad was always ready to well bless them. Whatever profit he made in his businesses, his first thought was to bless the Lord's work with it.

When I met Chris, as soon as my Dad found out that Chris's Dad was a pastor, and hadn't been able to pay his National Insurance Stamp for years, I was sent to the Post Office for reams of them. Dad paid them all right up to date for him. Then when Chris went to Bible school, it was my Dad who paid his fees.

This big cheque has jolted me. It has brought home that it is me, Dad's daughter, who is now on the receiving end. *We* had been the givers at our house. *We* had been the well off ones who helped everyone out. Although my Dad was a pastor, he was in business specifically to be able to bless the Lord's people and the Lord's work. He even paid for a brand new church to be built in Coseley, to replace Coseley's little old wooden mission hut in the field where I had been converted. My Mom also fostered, without pay. Whenever my Auntie Bessie was pregnant – yet again – and couldn't cope, my Mom would nurture several of my tiny cousins. They would live with us for months at a time.

We had been brought up to share, to give, to be generous, without a second thought. For the first time, I feel on the other end. I feel like someone else's responsibility. I question for the first time 'living in faith'. I am experiencing the unexpected emotion of feeling like a scrounger.

"Chris," I say, "don't you think that once we have used the gift for what it was sent for, we won't be real missionaries any more?" I had seen it all on missionary slides. The less the missionaries had, the more we admired them, and the more ashamed we felt for having things. Missionaries were the essence of spirituality, because of their ability to live a life of lack.

Since living in Cuevas, we have started to get visitors and I love it. They are missionaries who travel from one end of Spain to the other. We are just in the right spot for them to break their long hot journeys. Even though some are the ones who couldn't give us the 'official help', it doesn't matter to us. I look forward to them calling. Any journey here entails long drives in sweltering hot vehicles, on inadequate twisting roads, and anywhere to break an uncomfortable day is welcomed. I never have any warning when they will pass through, having no telephones, but they know I will always be prepared for them. We have become an established halfway mark, and I couldn't be happier about it.

So I choose this as my first reason to tell Chris about the money. "Chris, don't you think it will spoil everything? We have started to be accepted as real missionaries, and are being of use to other missionaries. We'll look like millionaires when they pass through if we use such a huge amount of money on ourselves. It will become tedious keep explaining 'the Lord provided'. If other missionaries don't have much, why should we?"

I have even just begun to get pleasure from wearing 'cast-off' clothing from the parcels. There are no shops so there has been no alternative. Once I did it, I received some satisfaction at feeling more like a missionary. It was a breakthrough after having always loved dressing up, and in my own personal taste.

"Chris," I try to explain, in case he hasn't quite realized the consequences. "It will get around how affluent we have become since visiting America. America will be used as the reason we have got rich. America is already being mentioned as a reason for make-up, and now two houses!"

One missionary had asked, "When we pass through next time then – where should we come for our welcome break – your country house or your town house?" I was utterly speechless, knowing the incredible story and provision behind it all, and had never seen the mission house and Cuevas, as having two houses.

The burden of the money has made me miserable. I don't want 'things'. I had 'things' when I lived with Mom and Dad. How I long for Chris to feel the same. But he'd never experienced a life of plenty. When he was growing up, his Mom even had to make him his clothes for Christmas presents. He had only known a life of lack; sleeping underneath the stairs so his Mom could use his room to take in visitors as his Dad's salary as a pastor was inadequate. That's why when it was Chris's turn to visit me in the Midlands from Fleetwood, it was like a holiday to him. He loved our abundance of food, centrally heated house, several vehicles on our drive – and going to our holiday house in Prestatyn.

I go over the contents of the letter again, that came with the cheque, and how it says that the entire gift must only be used on us personally, and "being the only reason it was given."

I start telling Chris my next reason. That even more than the missionaries thinking we are rich, how will we explain to our street of poor people why we have a fridge when they don't? Why we have furniture when they don't? Why we have a washing machine while they will still be washing on a pila?

I can't come to terms with the fact that the gift would be of any advantage to what we are trying to accomplish here, and think it will stumble the neighbours, making our witness a waste. If these people can't have things, I don't want them either. I don't want to go through trying to fit in – to destroy it all by doing something that I see as unwise.

But Chris can't help but feel thrilled about the gift, and

is unable to comprehend how I could throw a gift from God back in His face.

"Yes, but Chris," I say, "when the money is in the shape of things, people may not understand it as God's blessing. They may see it as missionaries being materialistic in a poverty stricken mission-field."

Chris explains how it may be nothing more than priorities. He says that some people may prefer their 'stuff' in a bank, rather than in the form of things, preferring to keep what they have private. Chris says he wants to see and enjoy what he has.

Then I tell Chris another one, hoping this one will really do it. I ask if it will matter to him when he doesn't look 'in need' any more, hindering any future financial help, as when we have used the money we certainly won't look in need, when we really could be – even if sitting on nice new chairs.

"Christine," he reminds me, "it may take faith – to enjoy."

But I still feel no excitement on our journey to the city to spend the money. No other gifts have come of late, so we have to start using some of the money to survive.

On the long journey to Malaga, a place we had heard had proper shops similar to England, I have time to think. I am thinking if it is even possible to be proud of a sacrificial lifestyle. A seed of sacrifice could be growing into a tower of pride.

I also think about living in faith and scrounging. I am reminded of Elijah, and how he 'scrounged' off a widow, asking her for her last bit of sustenance during a famine. I wondered if he had been embarrassed by it, or been criticized for it. During all this, I hadn't given much thought about the givers, and how the Bible says, "It is better to give than to receive." The Lord could want to bless the givers of our gift, more than us! It could be that the givers of our gift have needs that will be met too. The widow gave her last without any thought of what she would get out of it. Yet her need was met, and her son was raised from the dead.

The children are so excited going to Malaga, asking what they will be able to have, and keep talking about a two day stay in a hotel.

However, when we arrive, we are absolutely frozen! We have no coats and people are staring in disbelief as we walk wet windy city streets in summery flimsy clothing shivering to death, dashing from one shop to another to get dry. We had never thought there would be such a difference in temperature just a day's drive away.

In a shop, Wes, Cherry, and Calvin go berserk at the sight of real toys, cycles, and games. Chris's eyes are fixed on a television set. I see a fridge and can imagine ice cubes and cold 'gaseosa' in it. Then I lounge on a soft sofa. Then I see a table and chairs and can imagine us sitting around it to eat together as a family. It is all an acute reminder of how we lived in jolly old civilisation. Then we find real turkeys, all ready dressed like in England. We will be able to have a traditional English Christmas. We buy some real Christmas trimmings, which will be a change from making our own.

We all place our orders in each department of what each of us has chosen, and go home to await the delivery of it all.

Surprisingly, everything arrives on the exact day they promised it would, and just in time for the English Christmas. I am so thankful it is while everyone is at the little market at the top of the village. All the stuff will be safely tucked away in the house so I won't have the trouble of making excuses for it yet. Their Christmas is Kings' Day on January sixth, when three men dress in robes and crowns and ride through the streets on donkeys masquerading as the three Kings. They won't know any better when we have our Christmas on the twenty-fifth of December.

Christmas Day has arrived and I drop the shabby green blinds and lock the door of our tiny little nest. We sit on high back pine chairs, around a matching pine table, and all of us gaze at a big, brown, turkey in the middle; the first we have had in missionary land. We feel like millionaires, and I hope the givers really meant what they said, 'spend it ALL on ourselves' – because we have!

Outside are all the same usual noises of Cuevas, horns, moms, animals, while indoors, we are quietly giving thanks to the Lord together. It is our very first English traditional Christmas with turkey, toys, Christmas lights, and trimmings, connecting the children to their homeland.

Then we ask a very special blessing on the givers of our Christmas, and pray that their needs will be met, knowing theirs is the better part. When we have eaten our dinner, we all open our gifts.

Suddenly, children outside have heard the sounds of a television, and I dread the reaction. They bang on the door, and as I open it children dash inside and go berserk. I never expected our children to suddenly acquire so many friends. Then their moms appear and ask if their children can watch the big television with our children. The ice has been broken like never before.

To my astonishment, they all think it so exciting having English neighbours with 'stuff', and everyone wants to see it all! Our house has become everybody's Christmas. Our little meeting room is full of children, which gives me the chance to introduce Bible stories. Neighbours come back over and again, and begin to enjoy everything with us. We then discover something new about this race. They don't have much respect for people with nothing. 'Stuff' creates respect.

I couldn't believe I had been concerned about the neighbours, as though the Lord hadn't been. If God wants to use a dead civet cat, He will. If He wants to use a colour television set He can. I am just a lump of clay, and clay lets the potter do the deciding, and clay must remember in future – that clay can't object!

After reading a scripture in Psalms, I will be careful to enjoy God's blessing, "And he did not delight in blessing, so it was far from him." (Psalm 109:17)

It could take faith… to enjoy it, not hide it.
It could take faith… to enjoy it, not excuse it.
It could take faith… to enjoy it, not endure it.

I thank the Lord for opening my eyes, that there aren't two Gods; one for missionaries, and one for others, and that God has the right to bless whoever he chooses to,

"Whatever the Lord pleases, He does" (Psalm 135:6).

I have learned that living in faith isn't being a scrounger. If it were, Elijah was one. If it were – Jesus was one too. He requested a little boy to give up his lunch, when He could have spoken a picnic into being in the first place.

Jesus didn't deny anyone – no matter how poor – the rewards of being a giver. He stood by and watched a widow give her last mite, but didn't stop her dropping it into the box.

I now understand that the Lord gives certain ones the privilege of giving, and it is they – who are the honoured ones. It is they who will receive the greater reward, and it will be more of a reward than a new dining set, fridge, or sofa. Theirs will be a lasting imperishable reward – straight from the Master's hand. "It is more blessed to give than to receive." (Acts 20:35) "Give and it shall be given unto you." (Luke 6:38)

It could take faith… to share it, not hoard it.

It could take faith… to enjoy.

16

It Could Take Faith…
to suffer with those who suffer

Day after day, a black and white photograph of a grim steely faced dictator is projected on the television, accompanied by drab depressing music.

The music stops several times throughout the day for an announcement that Franco is still poorly.

Our home isn't filled with the laughter of children any more. There's nothing for the children to watch on T.V. All television programmes have been censored in respect of Franco's illness.

All the children are missing their favourite T.V. programme, 'Pippi Langstrom' (Pippi Longstocking), to which they had all become addicted. It is about the simple happenings of a little Swedish girl called Pippi who has long blonde pigtails and crumpled stockings that don't stay up. She gets up to some simple mischief every week. It was the highlight of the children's week. Even the most undisciplined of children would sit as quiet as mice waiting for Pippi's mischief to be discovered, and then the room would erupt with roars of laughter when it was. Cherry has another new nickname. As well as being called 'La Coqueta', she is called Pippi, because of her long blonde pigtails like Pippi's. The neighbours are also missing a favourite programme. They had been going wild about a new Spanish singer from Madrid called Julio Iglesias. He's a handsome Spaniard, but as far as talent goes, Chris and I don't get his lightweight quivery voice. However women are swooning over him.

As ever, the civil guards are spying on everyone while Franco is ill, checking reverence is being shown. No one even dare smile. Franco's illness has caused the same deathly atmosphere as the flood.

Two guards sit in our meetings, and right by the door, with their machine guns in full view. It intimidates anyone wanting to come in. At times we feel despairing and as if nothing is being accomplished. People freeze at the thought of sitting alongside machine guns. I wonder how much courage people from our country would have, to sit next to a guard with a machine gun, and just how faithful anyone would be under such conditions.

However, the gospel is still being sown in a place where it never has been – albeit over walls, or at a market place. I pray so much that souls will turn to the Lord. We haven't been swept off our feet with what we have seen in our ministry here yet. But we had been told by neighbours and some market-sellers how they would like to come to the meetings, and that they knew of others who would like to come too – but fear the Guards. If freedom ever does arrive in this country, I believe that there could be a surge of 'secret disciples'. Joseph of Arimathea and Nicodemus were secret disciples through fear.

As yet, it all seems to be sowing, and not enough

reaping, and that word sowing is becoming a new fear for me. Sowing isn't seen as successful as reaping.

Because of our tradition, we aren't content. I sometimes wonder if we have it all wrong, wanting to see some visible success to be able to point to.

One day, I am in the middle of my daily ritual of mopping from corner to corner and applying bug-powder – I just have to put up with the umpteen lizards in Cuevas which run up the walls and scare me to death. A special announcement comes on the television. I keep the television on all day to see when programmes will return to normal for the children. The children never stop running into the house with the same question, "Is Pippi back on yet Señora Cristina?"

The special announcement begins, in a cold, deep, and deathly tone: "Españoles – Franco ha muerto." (Citizens of Spain – Franco has died.) We can't believe it! They had been telling us for months that his condition wasn't at all serious.

The announcement goes on:

"A truly great man. Who for God and posterity gave his life with intense dedication in the fulfilment of his transcendental mission."

Unbelievable! A man who had been dictating every day, to 38 million people, what to do, how to do it, when to do it; a man who had told 38 million people what to think, how to think, and when to think it – or else. A man who had driven people to live in holes in mountains – and it is announced that he had done it for God!

Well now, he has gone to meet his Maker, and will have to answer for what he did for God.

We want to celebrate the news. But we are surprised when no one else wants to do it with us. We can't understand it, and I feel a fool thinking I must have misunderstood the announcement.

Yet I know what I heard. The announcement was quite simple, and my Spanish reasonable – I had actually been told that my accent was more authentic than Chris's, much to his embarrassment. But it was only because I could copy well. Chris has by far the greater vocabulary.

We begin to think that people just haven't heard the announcement about Franco, yet there are bars now that have a little television set, which are always the most crowded ones. The announcement had to have been heard.

But even when the news is well and truly out, there is still no joy. It is confusing. Everyone avoids talking to us about it, or only whisper. We almost have to pretend it hasn't really happened.

We wonder if they are waiting to be told when they can believe it. After never having been allowed to decide anything for themselves – perhaps they don't know where or how to begin. It is sad to see that through fear, they can't gain any satisfaction from this incredible news.

One day, we find out what the caution is all about. Somebody is kind enough to warn us. They say to be very careful because it is all a trick. That Franco isn't really dead at all. They say it is to spy on who would celebrate if he were! So Franco is dead, and they are *still* afraid.

The months roll on. The civil guards still line the streets. Things look exactly the same. So we start thinking they may be right. How is anyone to know?

One day, the drab depressing music constantly projected over the airwaves is a little bit shorter than normal. Then the wonderful deeds of Franco take a few minutes less on the television. Then a programme other than an official one comes on television – and it is this that portrays a miracle to the women. They are saying it hadn't been a trick after all.

Then a cartoon appears. Then 'Pippi' returns! Our house is full of the laughter of children once more.

Months and months after the dictator's death and there is some celebration showing 'por fin' (at last). There is a flurry of excitement, and it isn't because of a fiesta. There is a lightness in the air that things could be going to change after all.

The first real sign of freedom is something funny. Little 'Francos' are popping up on every street corner, each one putting the world right. Opinion expressing amongst the men becomes the height of fashion. Instead of just shouting their opinion in a bar, they now shout them in the street. They feel important and can express themselves without the fear of being thrown into prison.

It is new entertainment for our family, and we are in stitches watching such slight men of stature behaving like tough opinionated officials, flailing their arms and shouting on the street corners. We call them 'the street corner dictators'. But such bravado means – freedom is really here.

It feels strange being liberated in a country which has been a prison for forty years. They don't seem to know what to do with their freedom, or where to begin. We had only tolerated their way of life for seven years, they for forty. The thick ice is melting. We are all free! We all feel like shouting – "FRANCO HA MUERTO! FRANCO IS DEAD!" But none of us have got quite that much courage as yet.

We had been allowed to enter into these people's downtrodden lifestyles. We had been allowed to experience their restrictions, anxieties, fears, imprisonment and frustrations. We had been allowed the privilege to suffer a while with them, to be afraid with them, to endure with them, to weep with them.

The whole experience has taught me another new lesson. It has turned me off the 'victory-type' attitude people had back home in England whenever anyone was going through a trial. If anyone had a particular 'weep' that wasn't someone else's weep, they would be slapped on the back by some spiritual champion, and be told to, "Cheer up brother! Cheer up sister! Just get the Victory! "

"Weep *with* those that weep. Be of the same mind toward one another... associate (mix) with the lowly." (Romans: 12:15)

It doesn't just say to "weep". It says to weep "*with*". Not to weep from a sympathizing distance, but *with*.

I have learned something else about faith. That faith can often be weeping.

It could take faith... to suffer with those who suffer.

17

It Could Take Faith...

not to be afraid

One day, while we are working at the Centro, visitors arrive. A tall impressive young couple holding hands, looking deeply in love, introduce themselves as Marjory and Jeremy. He is a handsome blond hulk; his wife a striking blonde.

There had been no notification they were coming to visit us. They ask if Chris remembers them from Elim Bible School.

In America, Chris had spoken at an Elim Bible School class. After the class, quite a few students had gathered around Chris to express how they would like to visit him in Spain. Apparently, Marjory and Jeremy, Dutch Canadians, had been amongst them.

We are shocked when Marjory and Jeremy tell us that after landing in London from Canada, they had hitch-hiked from London right to our door. This trip is their honeymoon.

They ask if they can stay for a month. We happily agree, and it is super to have someone English to speak to, not to mention Christians, and the Centro will be occupied again. Marjory and Jeremy are like a cool fizzy drink on a boiling hot day. They are sharp and witty. We have never quite met anyone like them or anyone as lively, vivacious and charming – reminding us of our time in America. Chris and I feel short, old, plain, even boring in comparison.

In fact, I feel ancient alongside Marjory. I suddenly feel the last few years may have taken their toll. I have always admired beauty, as God's creation, not in a jealous way, but how everything was meant to be, until Eve spoiled it all. I used to watch programmes like Miss World, and most times chose the winner. I am convinced everyone will be flawless in heaven. I would love to have been a beautiful person, instead of hating mirrors and cameras. I am always concerned that if I loathe looking in a mirror while I am young, how will I cope with wrinkles, jowls, and thinning hair.

We are so enjoying Marjory and Jeremy's company. They are a breath of fresh air in Cuevas. Calvin is enamoured of them. It is unique to hear a Canadian accent in little old Cuevas. It is as if a light bulb has been switched on.

Marjory and Jeremy are thrilled to be able to stay in the Centro. It feels great having a mission house for the Lord's people, and I am so glad I left everything in it for the Lord's work.

Marjory and Jeremy's stay isn't quite over, but we are not surprised when they say they are leaving early. We are used to visits being cut short. It is a boring and uncivilised place unless one has a specific purpose to be here. Calvin is upset waving them off. They then surprise us by telling us the reason they are leaving early – to return home to get their belongings, as they have decided to return and be missionaries alongside us! We are stunned, but stop ourselves from getting over-excited as we have heard it all before.

We miss Marjory and Jeremy. They have been the best fun we've had since Pepe left. It has felt strange having other English speaking Christians to share with, laugh with, and especially someone to pray and discuss spiritual things with, and in the American-Canadian accent which takes me back to New York.

It would be the perfect lifestyle if they did return. We would be in Cuevas, and they could be in the Centro. We would be a group, a team.

We wait and wait for some word from them. There's nothing. We had really felt, more than any one else, that they would be the ones to keep to what they said. It is getting difficult not to build up our hopes about them coming back. As well as being full of fun, there was a serious dedication where the Lord's work was concerned. In Canada, they were house parents, and ran home fellowships.

In the meantime in Cuevas, things are starting to change. We are the very first foreigners here. They now feel a sense of pride that they have a British family living in Cuevas; who chose to live in their tiny insignificant place rather than by the seaside. We even discover a secret. That the opinion they have of the English is that they are dignified and upper class. There is a desire to make Cuevas better. First, Miguel's Mom comes to see me. She apologizes to me about the toilet door. She explains how they have decided to have it altered for our sake, so that the entrance will be from inside the bar. We are amazed when within days the job is completed. They even put a little fence up and climbing plants to hide the bar for us from our window.

Then one day, cement, floor tiles, gravel, and sand, all get tipped right outside our gate, reminding me of the days when it all arrived at the Centro. But no one has told us what it's all about, and as plans can change overnight, we could end up stepping over gravel and sand indefinitely. Chris can't seem to find out anything about it.

Then we fear it could be Pablo. What if it is still his house and he is going to do some alterations? What if we are told to leave because of some dodgy goings on about papers or payments?

My neighbours start to teach me many things, making me realize more than ever how they are not an unintelligent race, just a deprived one. They teach me how to knit without a pattern, how to crochet, how to make a delicious meal out of hardly anything, how to de-scale and dissect the weirdest of pink fish, how to pluck a chicken, how to crack pipas correctly, and how to put corn in a pan to make it into popcorn like we had in America. We are taken into the countryside where they make paella on a fire, so I can learn how to make it. Then a dear and ancient sweet lady crochets me a shawl, which is what every woman has around her shoulders in winter. The dear soul had noticed how I didn't wear one. It is in beautiful black and white fine hairy wool, which she has even bought herself. I have to wear it no matter how roasting I am even in winter. I am still reprimanded in winter when the children aren't in sweaters, scarves, and thick socks when playing outdoors, telling me how ill they will be. It is a race that still fears illness.

One day Pablo turns up, and our hearts miss a beat as he wants to take us to the agents. Although Chris had gone through a few nerve racking moments, the Lord had met every instalment. True to his word, Pablo presents us with a proper deed to say the house is ours! We see on the deed, that the real name of our street is 'Las Arenas' (The Sands), which seems strange when there isn't any sand or sea. Then Pablo tells us that all the materials outside the house are for a pavement in Las Arenas – the first street to have one. It is also going to be the first road to have tarmac. The work begins and finishes so swiftly we can't believe we're in the same Spain. They have even put in a street lamp. The street doesn't look like my little 'ditch' any more. Las Arenas looks posh to the rest of Cuevas. We are told how our family has had influence for the good in Cuevas.

Chris decides he will join in with all the new alterations in Las Arenas, and begins doing DIY again. He lays tiling over our own front dirt patch, going around the orange tree and lemon tree which were already in place. We now match the smartness of the new Las Arenas.

I can hardly take in how I had truly believed that when leaving England I would never ever live in another home, let alone own one!

My kindest neighbours are Pía and María, who have me around their houses regularly for coffee. They tell me how they want to teach me more of the gypsy culture. Gypsies don't seem too accepted by non-gypsies, so this is a great compliment to want to help me understand them better, as they have noticed how pre-occupied I am about getting a culture right. I have friends. The fear has gone at last. I am accepted, and have become a friend.

One day Chris and I are in a tiny 'Ferretería' (hardware shop). We are amazed to see lying underneath the counter amongst some screwdrivers, hammers and nails – a beautiful carved gold bracelet. I point it out to Chris thinking it can't be real, shocked not only to see such a piece of jewellery on sale here, but lying alongside tools. The owner of the shop picks up the bracelet, thinking I am interested in buying it, and urges Chris to buy it for me. We both decline, but ask why he is selling a gold bracelet in his tool shop. He explains that he is starting to build up a business and can only afford one piece at a time. He urges Chris to take it, and just to pay something on it whenever he can! He says, he knows and trusts who we are. To us, this is the ultimate of trust and acceptance. To my astonishment, ignoring all my objections, Chris tells the owner he'll accept the offer and gives the man a mere 1000 peseta note (£4) as a deposit and then asks the owner if he could engrave it with '12 años casados' (married 12 years). It is a twelfth wedding anniversary gift from my dear hubby, to mark not only our twelfth wedding anniversary, but to also mark real acceptance here at last, and to mark a real time of change in Spain. We are in with this one big family. We are even invited to the Mayor's house for a meal as well as other influential people. The fear really is a thing of the past.

One day, the villagers start walking towards the riverbed in Cuevas taking along picnics. We just think it is some Saint's day we have forgotten. But then people start congratulating us, saying, "Que Suerte Eh?" (How Lucky Eh?)

When we haven't a clue as to what they mean, they say, "You mean you don't know? You don't know what is going on and what it means for you?" When we admit we don't, they explain how the Spanish government has decided to undertake the biggest of projects in this corner of Spain. At terrific expense, they are making the riverbed safe!

So everyone is taking picnics to be able to stay and watch bulldozers and trucks, fascinated with all the huge equipment that has moved in. It is a massive happening, even to outsiders of the village, who are coming into

Cuevas to watch it all happening. In a place where nothing has ever changed, where nothing goes on, people just stand hour after hour watching a riverbed being dug out and reinforced. It will make flash flooding in Cuevas a thing of the past. People are so excited to see some progress, in their tiny insignificant Cuevas.

But it is our little house which is an even bigger talking point, as it is the only one level dwelling in Las Arenas. They refer to Pablo who sold us the house for peanuts, and was glad to get rid of it, and we have only just received the deed. Some are annoyed about it, others are pleased for us. They keep saying, "That little place you live in is now worth money!" Then people start asking us if we will sleep more peacefully when the riverbed is finished. Yet we haven't lost a night's sleep about the flood. The only time I remembered it was when neighbours gathered in groups worried, whenever there was a rare cloud in the sky.

--oOo--

One day when we go to the Centro, who should be sitting outside, but Marjorie and Jeremy! Just as before, we'd had no indication they were coming. They had brought their belongings just as they said they would.

Marjory and Jeremy aren't on honeymoon any more, and start throwing themselves into the work, and our work-load is halved. Everything is much easier with the four of us, and it is incredible working as a team.

The cave people freeze at the sight of Marjory's beauty with her blonde hair, pale skin, and cute Dutch nose. Marjory is unaffected, and not like I was at all. They are both so mature for their young twenty-one years, and are talented too. I have always been an admirer of talent.

Marjory and Jeremy are bright and picking up the language quickly. They are qualified child carers, so we arrange a camp at the Centro for underprivileged children. The children sleep at the Centro. The mission house has now turned into a children's Christian camp. Some of the children have travelled all the way from Murcia. Marjory and Jeremy do the catering, and it is the first time we have seen chips cooked with the skins still on. Marjory says it saves time. They conduct the meetings, and run around like kids playing all the games. These underprivileged children are overwhelmed to be having their very first Christian camp meeting, singing, and eating meals all together, never having experienced a holiday, never mind a Christian one.

Marjory and Jeremy love living in the Centro which is fully equipped for them. Then we feel to let them have the vehicle we use to transport villagers to the Centro for those too afraid of being seen in our village meetings.

To signify a time of liberation and change, we plant pine trees at the Centro. Chris tells me to put only one pine in each hole, on seeing I had put two in one hole, but it's because the pines are only the size of a matchstick.

Marjory and Jeremy preach, they sing, they play guitars, they teach. It is right, and natural to let them loose. We are a team and all in it together, sharing everything.

In the meetings, with Jeremy on a guitar, and me on the accordion, all of us singing together, the open air meetings are vibrant, and alive. The clapping of the gypsies makes it a pulsating and exciting time.

We order a Christian film in Spanish to show outdoors called 'Time To Run'. Chris and Jeremy make a massive outdoor screen. We borrow chairs from everyone and anyone. We put the film on night after night, and sing and make appeals. People, at last, start coming – walking from the villages. The police still watch everything we do, but at least we can get written permission for mostly everything.

We love Marjory and Jeremy, who are a spiritual couple, and who obey their call with enthusiasm. Such intense zeal can only be from God. It would be wrong to deny them any part in the ministry. They don't have children, and can dedicate every single second to the work.

At Christmas, we all decide we will give others some fun. We buy red cloth and cotton wool from the market, and make it into a Santa suit. We fill pillowcases with presents, and go to the caves on Christmas Eve. Jeremy is tall so he is the Santa with the bag of gifts over his shoulder. As we drive along people are stunned on seeing Jeremy, never having seen anything like it.

When we arrive at the caves, all the children are in bed, but the parents are so taken aback they let us go right into the back part of the caves where the children are sleeping, to wake them up. We are horrified to see them sleeping on tatters and old mattresses on cold dirt floors, and the place swarming in creepy crawlies and flying bugs. When we wake the children, they are amazed to see Jeremy dressed as a Santa with presents. They are overwhelmed on opening them.

After this we make special appeals to our families and friends abroad for bedding, sheets, and things for cave children.

Marjory and Jeremy hardly need any advice from us any more. They know the ropes well. One day, they want to tell us something special. They tell us that they know without doubt, that God has called them right here, and to the work we are doing, and ask if the Centro can be their home. Jeremy even asks for Chris's office at the Centro to write newsletters, print tracts, study, and so on.

We are overjoyed that someone else feels called here. It is thrilling to have people to work with. I start wondering again, why the Lord would have sent us at all. It had taken so long for me to be a missionary, and ready-made ones had arrived. Marjory doesn't even twinge at the sight of a bug, and isn't one bit squeamish. It seems neither of them had any adapting to do.

Then Chris and I suddenly see that we have given so much, tried so hard, shared so much – wanting to make them feel at home, useful and needed, as well as doing what is right by the Lord – that there is hardly anything left for us to do, and hardly anywhere for Chris to go. They are so competent we are starting to feel a little like on-lookers, or spare-parts.

We don't mention how we are feeling to Marjory and Jeremy, not wanting to displace or discourage them, but we wonder if they can sense our awkwardness.

It's easy to see that both Chris and Jeremy are born leaders, and both made to oversee a ministry, and shouldn't be sharing one in such a small place. I can see Chris looking a little disjointed, even a bit stagnant, and I have a frightful thought. I am afraid in case this talented, able young couple may not have been sent by God to work with us after all. I am afraid they may have been sent to replace us!

When I think, how long it has taken for us to make small dents and break the ice here, especially Calvin in two schools, and how long it has taken for me to be anywhere close to being a missionary, and to feel somewhat settled, I can't face any thought of being replaced. It has taken me too long to learn the ropes. I can't face another time of adjusting to somewhere else. Unlike my Mom, I hate being uprooted. I hate moving – probably because I had experienced it so much with Mom. Once I have found any bit of contentment, I cling, rather than take any risk of jumping from the frying pan into the fire.

I know Cuevas will be a dirty little hovel for decades to come. It would take years to change a long neglected area from a dump, even with a new pavement, street lamp, and reinforced riverbed. But it is still the children's home.

Also, we have just heard that we are going to have our telephone connected! A red telephone has been sitting in our lounge for months. We are just waiting for a connection date. I can't imagine the joy of answering a telephone in my own house again, to hear Mom on the other end asking to speak to her grandchildren.

We haven't seen a revival or anything close. Yet it would have been impossible to have done more sowing, more crying, more praying. I had truly prayed my heart out for souls – and for freedom.

So I am afraid. I am afraid of a scripture. The scripture that says, "One sows and another reaps" (John 4:37). I am so afraid that we are the 'one,' and that Marjory and Jeremy are the 'another.'

I just want to carry on serving the Lord with Marjory. I love her, and she me. She is a sweet and loving friend. I am willing to be in the background, to be *their* helper. There is nothing more we can give to this lovely couple now, other than ourselves. So we will be *their* assistants, *their* servants.

But alas, my 'authority' doesn't like what I have decided for us, and says something that sends me into a spin. Chris says he wouldn't be surprised if we have completed our work throughout all the caves and villages, and because Marjory and Jeremy feel called, we may need to leave the rest to them now.

Chris is of the opinion how it is now a free country. How there is a new government and a new King; a King who wants all things different for his country. Chris says that Christians and pastors will soon pop up everywhere and will reap a good harvest because of freedom.

On seeing my fear, Chris says, "God may have something else for us Christine. We don't want to look like 'hangers-on', The Lord has sent a capable couple. We won't be abandoning anyone." He explains that Marjory and Jeremy need to feel they are not being mollycoddled or overseen.

No matter how tough anything had been on the mission-field, there had always still been an inexplicable unspoken peace between Chris and I, that at least whatever we were going through, we were where God wanted us to be, doing what He wanted us to do. But something feels different. Chris talks of Paul the Apostle, who planted, sowed, and moved on.

I think about Abraham, "By faith Abraham... went out, not knowing where he was going" (Hebrews 11:8).

It could take faith... not to be afraid.

I start to think about the disciples and how afraid they were during a storm. I had never been able to understand why a group of robust fishermen would be afraid of one particular storm when they must have been in many a one. In this storm, they even had Jesus in their boat. They must have only just witnessed miracles too. Nevertheless, it was one storm in particular making their hearts pound. But fear is a natural emotion we were created with. It is normal to be afraid sometimes! So why would Jesus tell the disciples they had no faith just because they were afraid? I had noticed how Jesus had never associated fear with a lack of faith. He had always shown compassion to anyone who was afraid. He always understood saying, "Don't be afraid." As I read about the prophets, people of faith, and the great men of God, I notice how they had all experienced being afraid at some time; God always cared and understood. The same disciples had also been afraid at the Transfiguration. What did Jesus do? "Jesus touched them and said… 'Do not be afraid'" (Matthew 17:7). So it can't be a lack of faith to be afraid.

But the disciples weren't just afraid. Jesus was sleeping peacefully during a storm, and they felt He was leaving them to cope alone. They got annoyed. They got irritated, until their exasperation turned into an accusation, until it got to the point they said to the Master, "Do You not *care…?*" (Mark 4:38). It was one thing to be afraid, and one thing not to be able to sleep peacefully during a tempestuous time, but another to suggest the Lord didn't care about it. The lack of faith couldn't have been because of being afraid during turbulence. The lack of faith was doubting the Lord, doubting He was concerned.

I have been through many a storm on my missionary journey here. I had come out the other side soaked, yet spiritually healthier. Yet it is this particular storm making my heart pound. Now it is me in a wobbling tipping boat, with icy cold waves of fear washing over me, and the salt water of doubt landing in my lap, I don't want to make the same mistake as the disciples. I don't want to think, that even though I am afraid, that the Lord isn't concerned. I want to be able to have the normal emotion of fear, without accusing the Master of not caring about it.

It would be better still – to be able to be at complete rest during turbulence.

It could take faith… not to be afraid.

18

It Could Take Faith...

to remember

Calvin is almost thirteen years old, and quite the happy Spanish boy. Wesley is at school, but has not taken to it like Calvin. At playtimes, he stands with a little feel-sorry-for-me face pressed against the netting of the playground, waiting to be handed the playtime bocadillo.

Some days, I discover that Wesley hasn't even entered the school gates at all, and has just stood outside, too sad to go in. He is happy in Spain, and loves an outdoor life and his dogs, but hates everything about the school, especially the teachers and the language. He's not the type to tolerate the boredom like Calvin. Freedom hasn't yet eliminated the rituals in the classes, and Wesley has no time or patience with it. Cherry has to begin school soon and she too, is shy and timid.

While Marjory and Jeremy aptly take care of the Centro, printing the literature, and doing the cave visitation, we have taken the opportunity to travel to various places at the weekends, to try to find where the Lord would have us go next. But nothing is becoming clear. We go to the cities of Almeria, Malaga, Murcia, yet feel nothing for any of them. We can't stay in them long enough to make a proper assessment. The costs to stay are exorbitant. There isn't a Pablo with a silly offer, and there's no Francisco with any more cheap land. We see now just how ridiculously cheap our mini bungalow was compared to a city house. So we keep arriving back home to Cuevas weekend after weekend, no nearer knowing what our next step could be.

The more we are away at the weekends, the more useless we feel when we get back to Cuevas. Marjory and Jeremy are doing things their way, and making changes. They are bound to have their own style of doing things.

One thing is certain. Chris says that without doubt, we have to do something, and soon. But I would still be content just to be the Canadians' helpers.

Eventually, we decide we need to test a place for longer than a weekend, with the intention of praying while there. So we feel to choose Malaga. But the apartment, food, and everything costs so much more than what we are used to, so we have to leave early. We are really wishing we still had our little old caravan to be able to stay on a campsite. But a Spanish missionary in Murcia asked if he could have it to strip down and make into a trailer to transport his ministry equipment, so we gave it to him.

Marjory and Jeremy are well settled in the Centro, although Marjory is finding it isolated. It isn't that she cares about the dark, lizards, bats, or temperamental water or electricity. Marjory is just an intensely gregarious person, and has to be chatting to people from the time she gets up until she goes back to bed. She says she will never learn the language properly while living in a wilderness, but she is still busy making the Centro a home for her and her husband. She has bought cloth and made covers for our sofas and chairs in her favourite colour of brown, as I had everything in my favourite colour of blue. The Centro doesn't feel or look like ours any more. So we accept that we built it for the Lord's work, and feel privileged that it is being used for that.

In Cuevas, people are noticing we are away at weekends, and rumours have started. In a village, it is impossible to hide anything. If there is one thing I have never been able to get used to in village life, it is how they thrive on gossip, which I find useless, boring – even harmful. I've had to accept it as small community living.

However, one morning it is gossip gone too far. Our neighbour Maria comes around to ask us if she can buy our house when we sell it! Having seen what rumours do here has caused me to develop into a ridiculously secretive person. To me, gossip is making someone of too much importance. Although I have always been inward, and feel safer and more protected keeping my feelings and emotions to myself, I have now turned into what people would call a 'closed' person. I have been amazed at how Marjory and Jeremy are an open book. No matter how personal an issue, they're never embarrassed about anything. Marjory says I can come over as being over cautious. But living in the village has made me so. Yet I don't want it to grow into a mistrust of people, so I am pleased Marjory was honest enough to point it out.

Chris promises Maria that if we do want to sell the house we will tell her first. Her house is built on stilts and joined on to ours. She is worried that if ever we sold it to someone else, the buyer would build a second storey, which would block out all her side windows.

Because I am overly discreet, we haven't mentioned to the cave people that we have been looking for ministry elsewhere. They just think that we are letting Marjory and Jeremy find their own feet on weekends while we have been evangelizing in a few other places. Chris really feels they should know, but would like me to feel a bit more peace about it, knowing I have problems disappointing and discouraging people. I don't want to risk them feeling they don't matter to us, especially after what we had been told by other missionaries, and had found it to be true; if anyone opens their home to have meetings, to be very careful, as they become possessive. They explained how they can get hurt very easily if ever they feel they are not the most important ones to the missionary. I had walked on eggshells ever since, and is the reason I am so worried about telling them we may be going to minister elsewhere.

I have an idea that I want to tell Chris about at the right time. I know I could probably swing things my way, like any wife could. One lady in England had told me how she had taught her daughter how to have control without her husband even realizing it. She said, "Christine, there is a way of making your husband think it is he who's had an idea, then he'll want to do it." I had proved over and again, that if I do things a Biblical way, God sees me right. I don't like cunningness in women. The dictionary definition for cunningness is: to deceive in a clever subtle way. It is disloyalty.

I tell Chris my idea. I suggest to him that we don't move anywhere, but that we minister elsewhere at the weekends, and then come back to Cuevas during the week. The children could stay in the same school, and I could still be with Marjory. Chris says he will think about it.

One day, we get a visit from the pastor of the church in Murcia, the one to whom we had given our caravan. He knows nothing of our turmoil and situation, and we put him in the picture. He then reminds us how we came and pioneered during a tough non-democratic time in Spain, and how we went through the hardship that goes with being the first to arrive with the Gospel in a dictatorship regime. He says how he truly believes that we now need some kind of recuperation before considering starting another ministry elsewhere. He compliments us on having done a good job of sowing, but says he feels we should now take some time to seek the Lord about our future. It's that word 'sowing' again!

He says we have evangelized almost every cave and village in the region, and that now freedom has arrived, there is already starting to be an influx of evangelists and pastors.

All I can think of as he speaks, is, the 'one' and the 'another'. I didn't want to be just a sower. Nothing is seen for a sower's hard work and tears. I want to be the 'another'. The reaper! Reapers get to *see* something and are the ones who get recognition.

It is the bombshell the pastor drops next that is a shock. He asks if we have considered going back to our own country for a while!

We say how we have never thought that way, but Chris graciously thanks him for his advice. But I want to know more. I want to know why the pastor would think of England, and if it is because I look worn out. But he says it is because of what he has heard about England. How it was a country which sent out missionaries, but that it is now a country that needs them. He says he has heard that over the last few years, it is slipping away from God; churches are emptying; there is a need for evangelism, whereas Spain will soon be thriving with national pastors, and evangelists. He says it is our own country that needs the Lord right now.

We are using a lot of petrol, running here, there, and everywhere, yet still feel no guidance, and feel more and more like spare parts as Marjory and Jeremy enjoy their new missionary experience. But we know we could never return to England. For one thing, Chris has built up years of trust and credibility with people who have helped us survive our missionary life of 'sowing'. It would be disloyal to them. We wouldn't be seen as missionaries in our own country, even if missionaries are needed there now. And I can never imagine our children being in the confines of England again, in a 'be-seen-and-not-heard' country. They are carefree little street kids, not to mention the sun they take for granted every day.

I don't know if it is what the missionary had said that had worked on Chris, but he is so frustrated one day after another fruitless journey to a city, that he blurts out, "Christine, we can't go on like this any longer, I am going back to England, and especially so if my own country is slipping away from God!" I am horrified. I immediately have to know how he knows it is God who has spoken to him, and why he feels that way.

Whenever Chris has an idea, or a plan, I always feel I should bring up everything I can think of, just in case there is one thing he hasn't thought through. Then, once I know he has seen every aspect, I leave him to it.

It isn't because I love Spain. I don't think as long as I live, that I could ever like un-kept barren wide open spaces, rubbish blowing everywhere, dust, unrelenting heat, flies, scorpions, wild dogs, and Civil Guards. It would take decades to tidy such a time warp, but I had settled those things long ago. It is where we had chosen to spend the rest of our days. It is where the children have pals. It is where we had been called to.

If we return to England, we won't be missionaries any longer. But what we would be – is failures, and losers. Anything less than returning from a mission-field in a coffin, or before one is 80 years of age, is falling short of the requirements of the utter dedication of a real true missionary. No matter what commendable work the Lord may have us do in England, we would never ever be forgiven for falling short of a call, and especially by those who had supported us. We may as well be backsliders, like 'the dog who has returned to his vomit.' I know our poor Moms would cringe with embarrassment, and I feel it would be letting them down, and everyone else too. But I almost die on the spot when Chris tells me where he is considering starting another work. WOLVERHAMPTON – of all places!

Wolverhampton is right where my Mom would have to face her church and all her friends. It would embarrass her to death, not to mention it is where I come from. Chris has taken me all the way to Paradise – to America, and we are now recognised missionaries – just to take me right back to Wolverhampton.

Yet, every spanner I throw in the works, Chris can only explain how he now feels that God is in our returning home.

When we were called to be missionaries, God had graciously spoken to me from Hebrews 11. Yet this time, I feel nothing, except uncertainty. So as God works through authority, and Chris is mine, I realize that I may not have to 'feel' anything. Thankfully, the responsibility isn't mine; mine is to obey. If the King of Kings could obey, and was 'obedient' even to the death of the cross – who am I to feel that obedience to a husband is beneath me?

I know it will still be a future of being asked the same questions, "What happened then? Why did you have to come back? Didn't it work out for you then?" The words 'losers' and 'failures,' could be our "thorn in the flesh!" I can hear the Lord already saying, "My grace is sufficient..."

In Gracia's cave one night she says, "Cristobal, have you found anywhere else to minister yet?" Chris is upset and embarrassed that we hadn't said anything to them as yet, and I feel I have failed him and them because it is my fault. Then Gracia asks, "Have you considered God may be sending you back home to do something in your own country?" Then Gracia starts to cry when we say we have thought about it. But she assures us that they will all be all right because the Lord has sent Marjory and Jeremy to take care of them, but she is sad.

--oOo--

One day our neighbour comes around and requests some privacy. She asks us to lock the door. She puts her hand inside her overall pocket and starts pulling out huge bundles of crinkly notes all rolled up tightly with an elastic band. She says, "I will buy your house, today, this very moment, here and now. Is this enough?"

We haven't a clue how much she is holding, but we have never seen so much cash in our lives! We don't even have a clue how much the house is worth. She starts unrolling the notes. They are so curly they won't stay flat on Chris's hot hand. They keep popping up, and she keeps on flattening out each one over and again.

She says, "Listen, I have made all the necessary enquiries of what the house is worth to save you the trouble of doing it. But I am going to give you more. I'll put it into piles of tens for you, and then we'll know where we are up to."

She continues, "I don't want to live in it of course. It's too small. I just want it to store my produce, but mainly it's because the house is joined onto mine. I could have bought this place years ago for nothing, like you did. But now the riverbed and street repairs have made it valuable, I have to pay the price for it, don't I? I assure you that I am going to give you more than anyone else would give you, because I have to have this house. Now, don't look so worried, there's no rush to go anywhere. Just stay in it as long as you like." Then she asks matter of fact, "Is that enough?"

Chris manages to squeak out a little, "Yes, yes," breathless at the sight of the stack of money in his hands. "Shouldn't we have someone here to witness and record this Señora?" Chris asks.

"No. No. Of course not, I trust you implicitly Cristobal. We'll just shake hands on it! One of the days we'll go to the Notaria together for a proper document to say the house is mine."

As she reaches the sum of 1 MILLION pesetas (£4,000) all in separate piles, Chris and I are like zombies. "That's it!" She says. "Is that enough? I want to make sure that I will give you more than anyone, and I think I have. The house is now mine right?" and she reaches out to shake our hands – then walks out.

Chris and I are speechless. We have never seen so much money in our lives, even from my Dad.

Then Chris throws all the notes onto the settee and shouts, "1 MILLION PESETAS Christine!!" Our tiny little mud filled flood house has made a total of 4 times what we paid for it; all because the Lord had reconstructed a riverbed.

We can't help the feelings of elation at the sudden appearance of £4,000. The money has certainly helped with the shock that we would be returning to England broke.

Maria had said there is no rush for us to leave, as she has only bought it to store vegetables in it.

However, after a while, Chris feels the urge to begin his new ministry and is anxious to get on with it after having made the tough decision to go. It all seems a waste of time to stay any longer. Yet I still want to hang on for as long as possible.

Then someone else calls to buy the house! We tell them it is too late. When they ask how much we have sold it for, they laugh at us saying, "It is worth more, and we will give you more." When we tell them we have promised, they keep telling us "son locos" (you are stupid).

Then, out of the blue, someone turns up to buy our vehicle with more cash! Then within days people are arriving pulling grubby money from aprons, skirts, shawls, pockets, to buy all our furniture, fridge freezer, beds. The children's toys are literally grabbed and money pushed into our hands. It is a great insight that these people did have money after all. There just wasn't anywhere to spend it or anything for them to buy with it. Now our house is a shop and they are fighting for our stuff.

We can hardly believe that in 24 hours everything is gone. I had never expected it to be so hard to give up things again. I had started to get attached once more, clinging again to places and possessions, viewing everything as permanent. I am determined that I will always be grateful whenever the Lord provides and enjoy it. But from this day I will always look on places and things as temporary.

The only thing to do now is to leave, and quickly. Cherry never did have the chance to start school.

Never again would we dither. Now we hardly have time to breathe.

Marjory is a very strong and resilient person, and I had never seen her cry once, but she stands weeping uncontrollably in Las Arenas, outside our empty house,

Jeremy cradling her in his arms, trying to be of comfort. They promise to look after the mission house. We are happy for them to continue living in it.

On the plane, at the sight of the scorched brown barren mountainous region beneath, all the memories suddenly overwhelm me, and I can't stop sobbing and shaking. I feel I will never get over it. We have to admit, we didn't see as much response as we had liked for all the labour we had put in. I won't blame anyone for expecting it to have been a lifetime call. I had too! I do however question, if it is 'holding up the traditions of man as the commandment of God' to stay in a place for a lifetime just because that is what had always been done.

"You nicely set aside the commandment of God in order to keep your tradition" (Mark 7:9).

Also, doesn't the Bible say it is better to obey than sacrifice? Well, at least, I am obeying – Chris.

How will I cope with the rejection though? Will the Lord meet our needs? Where will we live? Will I ever get to go to America again, not being a missionary any more? Will Calvin be able to settle and be accepted in an English school at nearly fourteen years of age?

I feel like David when he was meditating in his sorrow, "Will He ever be favourable again? Has His promise come to an end? Has His loving kindness ceased? Has God forgotten to be gracious? Has He withdrawn his compassion?"

Then I said, "It is my grief…I shall REMEMBER the deeds of the Lord." (Psalm 77:7-11)

It could take faith… to remember.

Epilogue

I am of the opinion that God isn't really concerned about what I can accomplish. After all, He made me. I arrived after He'd done it all!

Whatever could I accomplish that God couldn't do without *me*. "Neither is He served by human hands as though He needed anything, since He himself gives to all life and breath and all things." (Acts 17:25).

"Heaven is My throne...earth My footstool. Where is a house you could build for Me? ...for My hand made all these things." (Isaiah 66:2)

So had it all been tests? "God led you in the wilderness... that He might *humble* you, testing you, to know what was in your heart" (Deuteronomy 8:2).

I am beginning to notice how there is a strong connection between *humility* and *faith*.

Jesus said to Mary, "Your faith has saved you," (Luke 7:50). What had Mary done? She had wept with uncontrollable feelings of unworthiness: humility.

To the Centurion Jesus said, "I have not found so great a faith in Israel," (Matthew; 8:8). What had he done? He had requested Jesus not enter his home: humility.

To the Canaanite woman Jesus said, "Your faith is great." (Matthew 15:28). What had she done? She had likened herself to a dog hoping for a crumb from His table: humility.

Humility always moved the Lord to respond – yet He called it faith.

I am just thrilled to see that there is *something* that can move the Almighty on our behalf; *something*, to cause the King of Kings, the Lord of Lords, the Creator of the universe – to pay attention to US!

"To *this* one I will look, to him who is *humble*..." (Isaiah 66:2).

"God is opposed (against) the proud..." (James 4:6). So perhaps God can't answer the prayer of someone He is opposed to?

"Whoever humbles himself as this child, he is the *greatest* in the Kingdom of heaven," (Matthew 18:4).

But how do I '*be*' humble?' How do I '*get*' faith?

"Faith (humility?) comes from... the Word of Christ." (Romans 19:17).

Reading His Word does something unexpected and special. It gradually unfolds God's unspeakable Holiness, His true perfection, His amazing massiveness, His infinite wisdom – to such an extent – it inevitably brings about feelings of awe and lowliness; and an unbearable and overwhelming view of the smallness of one's self. It makes one identify with Job who said, "If I called...I could not believe He was listening to *my* voice." (Job 9:16).

David called himself a nobody, ("I am small and despised" Psalm 119:130), God had a soft spot for him, because he was a serious delighter in God's word. Also David humbly repented of every mistake he made – paying the huge price and consequences of each, never to repeat the same. Some people can never forget a mistake, yet through David, God shows He is the God of the second chance.

David's priority was God's word: "I shall delight in Thy statutes. I shall not forget Thy word. Thy law is my delight. If Thy law had not been my delight, I would have perished in my affliction. Trouble and anguish have come upon me; yet Thy commandments are my delight. I rejoice at Thy word as one who finds great spoil." (Psalm 119:16, 77, 92,143).

My Prayer:

Dear Lord,

I had wanted to be the perfect missionary. I had wanted to be the perfect Christian wife, mother, woman – but you graciously moulded me into what you wanted. As painful as it had been at times Lord, I wouldn't want it any other way.

Although I felt at times, that I was often on the Potter's wheel going around and around, being pummelled and squeezed, I am aware that if I am to end up the design of the vessel you have in mind for me, that there will always be a need for re-shaping or re-correction.

Lord, I want to mean the words of that old chorus – "Have Thine own way, You are the Potter, I am the clay, mould me and make me…" so I must expect to be thrown into a spin on occasions – if I want to be a vessel for honour – and at least the spin will confirm I am loved.

Amen

"For those whom the Lord loves, He disciplines (exercises, chastens)" (Hebrews 12:6). "Blessed is the man whom Thou dost chasten" (Psalm 94:12). "Blessed is the man You discipline" (Psalm 94:12). "No discipline seems pleasant at the time, but painful, later...it produces... righteousness and peace" (Hebrews 12:11).

At least I know – that when I am on the wheel of the Potter – I am privileged. I am privileged because I have the full attention of the Potter!

"There are not only *gold* and silver vessels, but also vessels of wood and *earthenware,* and some to honour and some to dishonour." (2 Timothy 2:20)

I want to know the difference between earthenware and gold.

Earthenware: It is a low-fired clay, so has to be fired on a *low* temperature; it cannot stand the *heat;* other clays can be fired to a temperature high enough to *mature* and *harden* them; earthenware is the cheapest form of ceramics; it is a more common vessel; it is porous.

Gold: It is a remarkable *rare* metal; it is called the *noble* metal; there is a *'gold standard test'* for its genuine value; it can withstand the hottest furnace and comes out of the fire refined; it is the only metal that doesn't form oxide film which means it will never rust or tarnish; it can be *hammered* so thin – that light can shine through it. Gold is a protector from *heat and radiation.*

The difference is DURABILITY. Whatever test gold goes through – it comes out more refined still.

However, I must always remember something – that... "All that glitters – is not gold."

"If I *speak* with the tongues of men and of angels...*have* the gift of prophecy...*know* all mysteries and knowledge... *have* faith to remove mountains...*give* my possessions to the poor...*deliver* my body to be burned – but do not have love – it profits *me* nothing, and I am nothing.

"Faith, hope, love... these three; but the greatest of these is love." (I Corinthians 13:13)

It could take faith... to love because love keeps on loving ("never fails/stops"). (I Corinthians 13:8)

I may have been growing faith in the desert – but what use will it be in a green and pleasant land like comfy old England?

To be continued...

Christine age 20 months

Chris & Christine's wedding

Caves in Cuevas

A Spanish Paella made by Christine

The Civet Cat